Giving Back

Giving Back

A Lifetime of Service to Kansas and the Nation

EDWARD F. REILLY JR.

WITH

CONNIE PARISH

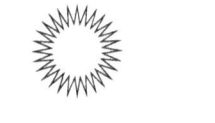

UNIVERSITY PRESS OF KANSAS

© 2025 by the University Press of Kansas
All rights reserved

Published by the University Press of Kansas (Lawrence, Kansas 66045), which was organized by the Kansas Board of Regents and is operated and funded by Emporia State University, Fort Hays State University, Kansas State University, Pittsburg State University, the University of Kansas, and Wichita State University.

Library of Congress Cataloging-in-Publication Data

LCCN 2025019710
ISBN 9780700640348 (paperback)
ISBN 9780700640355 (ebook)

British Library Cataloguing-in-Publication Data is available.

Authorised Representative Details: Easy Access System Europe
Mustamäe tee 50, 10621 Tallinn, Estonia | gpsr.requests@easproject.com

Cover design by Karl Janssen
Photograph: Portrait of Edward F. Reilly Jr. as US Parole Commissioner. Department of Justice photo.

These memoirs are dedicated with love and respect to my parents, Edward F. Reilly and Marian Sullivan Reilly, whose influence and encouragement have been so critical in my public life and service.

It was their conviction and ethics that provided my road map through life by teaching me to share my love for others, and to use wisely the many opportunities I had to serve. My prayer is that.

The book is also dedicated to my sister Mary Ann, my brother Jerry, and my son Joseph. After all, I may not have finished it had Joseph, when he was thirteen, not said, "Dad, you need to write down what might be helpful to others, since you have experienced so much."

Contents

Foreword   ix

Preface   xiii

1. How It Began   1

2. Entering the Public Square   25

3. The Issues   44

4. Capital Punishment   55

5. The Lighter Side   71

6. Life Experiences   78

7. Our Love Story   91

8. Having Children   103

9. Close It Down   107

10. Being Chairman   118

11. Looking Back at the USPC   139

Contents

12. Association of Parole Authorities International   148

13. Why Parole?   155

14. My Mentors   159

15. Sex, Scandal, and Lies   164

16. History of the Parole Commission   169

17. Where Do We Go from Here?   174

18. Public and Private Life Intersect   181

19. Ten Masters   191

20. Defenders of the Faith   201

Acknowledgments   209

Foreword

Giving Back is Kansas senator Edward F. Reilly Jr.'s story of growing up in the Midwest, first reaching the state capital as a legislator and then the nation's capital as a political appointee.

Born and raised in Leavenworth, Kansas, Ed Reilly was fascinated from an early age by the maximum security penitentiary twenty blocks from his home. He begged his father, the mayor of this historic community, to figure out how he could tour it as a gift for his fourteenth birthday.

Fast-forward to the day in the early 1990s when US Senator Bob Dole from Kansas asked Ed what qualified him to be chairman of the US Parole Commission. Ed was able to cite his navigation through twenty-nine years of Kansas politics, including leadership of a powerful committee heavily involved in correctional issues. He'd also repeatedly spearheaded a capital punishment bill, making him the governor's natural choice when he wanted two legislators to scrutinize the hanging of Perry Smith and Richard Hickock, who had cold-bloodedly murdered a western Kansas farmer, his wife, and their two teenage children. Smith and Hickock caught the attention of author Truman Capote, who chronicled their exploits in his nonfiction novel, *In Cold Blood*, a bestseller made into a movie. Reilly stood beside Capote, also a witness to the executions, during that rainy, gloomy night in 1965, at the gallows in Kansas State Penitentiary in Lansing.

Senator Dole knew Ed had successfully maneuvered other legislation that helped change the landscape of the state, including liquor by the drink, gambling, and pari-mutuel betting. He recognized that Reilly was a shrewd businessman, a principal in the realty and insurance business his father and grandfather founded in the 1920s.

So, the US senator—who aspired to the presidency himself—figured he and the rest of the Kansas delegation could make a strong case to President George H. W. Bush that Reilly could handle the chairmanship of the federal parole agency.

And that's how Mr. Reilly came to Washington where he faced his most difficult challenges in both his professional and private life. Professionally, he had strict orders to phase out the US Parole Commission within five years, since Congress had mandated it be replaced with the US Sentencing Commission. The latter agency operated on the principle, "If you do the crime, you do the time," with no consideration of a life changed for the better within prison walls.

Personally, his twenty-five-year love story with Luci Slattery came to a tragic end. Their son, Joseph, was born only six months before Luci died of complications from cystic fibrosis, and Ed faced the stark reality that he was a single father. He was left with memories of their fifteen-year marriage and regret that they hadn't wed ten years earlier when they were first introduced.

Yet he managed, bolstered by the faith that took root in his childhood, even when Congress was forced to extend the agency for years. That was prompted by the closing of DC's infamous Lorton Correctional Complex and changes in military incarceration, resulting in the transfer of thousands of military prisoners to the Bureau of Prisons. Since many of these prisoners would become eligible for parole, the agency had to remain to perform that service.

After serving on the Parole Commission, Reilly was US Observer to the International Fund of Northern Ireland, a position he held for two and a half years during the Trump Administration. He attributes that position to the relationships he developed with Irish military officers who attended the Command and General Staff College at Fort Leavenworth. Today he remains active in the matters of his ancestors' native Ireland as well as weighing in on criminal justice matters currently facing the country.

All of this involved serving those whom Ed considered his "masters," five Kansas governors and five presidents, all the while recognizing the ultimate Master who influenced his life and whatever success he attained.

Ed hopes his autobiography will encourage others to engage in service to their country and use the lessons he learned to benefit their fellow men and improve the world. His association with Senator Bob Dole and his admiration of Dole's service prompted him to establish the Edward F. Reilly Public Engagement Fund at his alma mater, the University of Kansas. This is an effort to encourage other men and women to make the sacrifice and enter the public square. Some of the engagement funds have also been extended to the Dole Institute, which is doing its part to educate students about the importance of public service.

Connie Parish
Leavenworth, KS

Preface

Writing down life's lessons is more challenging than I imagined. For a long time, I put off even starting, worried about the immense time commitment and my ability to recall everything I wanted to share. It was my son, then thirteen, who convinced me when he said, "Dad, you need to write down what might be helpful to others, since you have experienced so much." I realized then I couldn't shirk my responsibility. Entrepreneur and motivational speaker Jim Rohm said, "A life worth living is worth recording," so I shall attempt to share my own experiences and those of colleagues with whom I had the privilege of serving.

With the assistance of Connie Parish, my aim is to reconstruct experiences that will be helpful to those who aspire to enter public life or the criminal justice field. At the end of our life, we have to ask: *What have I contributed, shared, or left that others might benefit from my life?* When I began writing this autobiography, I had to ask myself this question. Despite the difficulty of carving out time from daily life, during my forty-seven years in the public square, I think I have learned a great deal in many areas—from business to politics to semi-retirement, when I've served on school endowment boards and condo associations. All have equipped me with invaluable insights.

Most people I know say they're going to write a book about their experiences, but never do. I made up my mind that I'm going to do this, and you can decide whether it's scrap for note-taking or helpful as you go through those remaining years of your life.

Either way, I believe my son was right. We all have a duty to be helpful to others. No matter how small or big a contribution we can make, we should make it. So let's you and I, together, go ahead to where my life began, and where yours might go.

1

How It Began

On my fourteenth birthday, my father asked me what I wanted as a birthday present. Without hesitating, I said I wanted to visit the prison—not just any prison, but the US Penitentiary in Leavenworth.

Leavenworth, the oldest city in Kansas, is the home of the first US penitentiary, built by territorial prisoners from Fort Leavenworth, about three miles away. My whole family was shocked at my request, but I'd always had a strong desire to see who was inside this magnificent structure that looked a lot like the US Capitol or some statehouse.

Getting permission to tour a maximum security federal prison in 1950—especially at my age—was not easy. But my dad was a close friend of the warden, Walter Hunter, who represented his title well. The two things I remember about him are the stogie in his mouth and his large black hat, which gave him a commanding presence.

The warden pursued the request with the US Bureau of Prisons, and to my knowledge I was the only boy in Leavenworth allowed to enter those front gates after climbing the forty-two imposing steps to the first gate. Neither my father nor I could ever have guessed how significant that March day would be. We would not have suspected that about four decades later I would be heading the panel that made life-altering decisions for inmates destined for parole or more years inside those walls. President George H. W. Bush appointed me as chairman of the US Parole Commission in 1992.

I realize now I gained wisdom and a more realistic view of prison by having this experience so early. I doubt it was a random event, though I might have thought so at the time. Now I wonder if it could have been the first step of a predetermined roadmap into the criminal justice system. But at the time, I never would have thought I would end up working in public service and, specifically, in anything related to our criminal correctional system.

And on that March day, walking up those steps was a moving, humbling, and even scary experience, especially since I suspected the prisoners might have catcalls for me. As we entered the first gate, we were immediately inside a cubicle portioned off by another gate. Upon identifying ourselves, we were admitted to another cubicle, which led into a general office where we signed in. The technology at that time was not as sophisticated as it is today, but our photograph was automatically taken prior to us being allowed to go into the prison.

Then, we stepped back into yet another cubicle after another gate opened. We were there until a fourth gate opened, allowing us to enter a giant rotunda—similar to what we have in the United States Capitol. The series of gates opening and closing sure makes you feel like you're leaving one world to step into another one. As we proceeded down the corridor, there were cell blocks off each side of the rotunda—four, as I recall. Prisoners were lined up along that wide expanse of hallway. As you might expect when someone goes into a prison—the catcalls started. I vividly remember some of the men saying, "Oh my heavens, we're going to have a young boy coming in here!"

At fourteen, I thought how frightening it would be to go into a place like that to serve with guys who obviously had other ideas regarding a young boy in their midst. It was a frightening experience for me, just visiting. Many years later, realizing the impact it had on me, I wanted my son Joseph to visit the Kansas State Penitentiary and the county jail. He was introduced to both during his formative days in grade school. I am pleased to say this introduction to my version of "Scared Straight" has, to this point, resulted in Joseph being a gentleman who has stayed out of trouble.

My experience also served as a great education because I visited the prison industries. I learned that, in most cases, the prisoners were able to work in the federal prison industries. I was surprised to see people learning woodworking, learning how to sew clothes or make shoes. Over time, this operation has become more sophisticated in our institutions, and today, some prisoners at the state prison in Lansing are working for three manufacturers in downtown Leavenworth—Zephyr, Heatron, and Henke—to make plows for commercial snowplows, electric heating elements used in restaurants and other food service venues, and parts for other equipment, among other items.

Since the early days, Leavenworth has been known as a "prison community." We first had the state prison, then the territorial prisoners at Fort Leavenworth built the federal prison. Now we have United States Penitentiary Leavenworth; Lansing Correctional Facility; the US Disciplinary Barracks at Fort Leavenworth, the military's only maximum security facility; the Midwest Joint Regional Correctional Facility, which houses military inmates serving sentences up to five years; and until recently, the Leavenworth Detention Center, a private facility that contracted with the US Marshals. So Leavenworth is a community that depends heavily on competent people in the corrections and criminal justice system, as well as people engaged in the security, protection, and defense of our country at Fort Leavenworth, which the Army considers their university.

The United States Penitentiary at Leavenworth is well known for incarcerating some of the most infamous criminals our nation has produced, including Machine Gun Kelly, Al Capone, the Bird Man of Alcatraz, Baby Face Nelson, and Leonard Peltier. Leonard Peltier is well known to people of my home state. He was convicted in 1977 of brutally killing two FBI agents on the Pine Ridge Reservation in South Dakota while they were investigating a crime that had occurred there. President Joe Biden commuted Peltier's sentence on January 20, 2025, to home confinement. He is now at the Turtle Creek Reservation in North Dakota. His first parole hearing occurred in Leavenworth on December 14, 1993, and the Parole Commission denied his application. My Leavenworth home was firebombed four days later.

As my public service journey proceeded, I was impressed by the opportunities provided to inmates at Leavenworth. Because of the federal system, they had the chance to get vocational training and partake in mental health services. If they were willing, prisoners were provided the tools to turn their lives around. At that time, all the elements were present to enable such a change.

But there's another side to the inmates' lives. Most people who have had any experience with correctional facilities know that most prisons are "colleges of crime." Those who end up there become better criminals than when they entered prison, because they learn the latest ways to manufacture drugs, break into a safe, or avoid detection by the law. More tragically, some don't ever make it out. Every time I remember seeing those four cell blocks on my Leavenworth trip as a child, I can't help but think of the higher tiers of those cell blocks from which many inmates were thrown by other inmates—either because they didn't do what they were told, or they didn't fall in line. I am aware of four such incidents that occurred during my time in the Kansas Legislature.

From the time I entered the Legislature in 1964 to 1992, there were twenty-three murders at the state prison. They were committed by prisoners burning one another to death in the cells, to stabbing one another in the showers, to beating people to death with a baseball bat. Whatever they could put their hands on to use as an instrument of death, they used. If they had to put something in a sock and beat a fellow convict's brains out with it, they did it. Inmates working in the machine shop put bolts in socks to use in fights. You can easily get murdered in prison for not complying. Prison has its own internal code of conduct and ethics, and you're expected to live by them. I would be grappling with this duality of environments within our prison system for quite a few years to come.

* * * * *

It is impossible to point to just one or two things in our lives that may determine what calling we choose. Everything we experience contributes to our decisions, our paths, our understanding of what our place and our role is. All in all, the "birthday trip" definitely sparked in me a curiosity about our criminal justice system. It would become a recurring topic for me even in my political science classes at the University of Kansas. I was inspired by my father; by Dwight D. Eisenhower, a fellow Kansan who was in the White House during my formative years; and by people like Frank Carlson, Bob Dole, and Nancy Kassebaum, US senators from Kansas. The lessons had a common thread: that our duty is not only to offer our talents and our leadership to those around us who need them, but to do it in such a way that we're able to capture their knowledge, their friendship, and their support. That is what defines a leader.

* * * * *

As I think about the wonderful life I have had in public service, I return to the influence that my hometown, my parents, and my family had on me. That hometown of Leavenworth, nestled on the west side of the Missouri River, was a great place to grow up. Everywhere you'd go, whether around the veterans' hospital or Saint Mary College (now the University of Saint Mary), you'd run into marvelous folks from all walks of life.

In its early days, Leavenworth was a thriving industrial community, the home of many of the nation's original corporations producing heating stoves, furniture, grain-sifting machines, and some of the first Ferris wheels, as well as woodworking and a mill-machinery plant. It's also the home of Fort Leavenworth, home of the US Army's Command and General Staff College, a Professional Military Education facility for US and international military officers. We were blessed to have many military families whose children attended our schools and brought an international perspective to the neighborhood.

In my travels, I've learned that most with even a cursory knowledge of history are acquainted with Leavenworth. The military leaders trained at Fort Leavenworth have gone on to be chiefs of staff, ambassadors, and secretaries, including some of the most famous: General Colin Powell; General and former President Dwight D. Eisenhower; Medal of Honor recipients Colonel Roger Donlon and Charles Hagemeister, both Leavenworth residents; and General Carl Vouno. Stepping back in history, there was General George Custer, famous for the Battle of Little Bighorn where he made his last stand against Lakota and Cheyenne warriors. Leavenworth was a major destination on the Santa Fe and Oregon Trail, which played an important role in the establishment of peace on the frontier during our country's Westward Expansion.

Fort Leavenworth was founded by an illustrious soldier, Henry Leavenworth. He was active in the War of 1812 and after that, his early expeditions were targeted at the Plains Indians. While on duty in the Midwest, he established several military forts, including what became Fort Leavenworth in the Kansas Territory. Two years after he was promoted to brigadier general, on May 8, 1827, he established *Cantonment* Leavenworth.

After successfully commanding the entire southwestern frontier, Henry Leavenworth died of a fever in July 1834. Initially buried in a simple soldier's grave at Cross Timbers in Indian Territory, where he died, General Leavenworth's body was transferred to a grave in Delhi, New York. But that was not his final resting place. A movement began in 1901 to bring him back to Fort Leavenworth. The War Department eventually sanctioned the move, and he was recognized with a twelve-foot granite monument in the Fort Leavenworth National Cemetery. He will always be remembered in this area, as not only the fort, but also the city of Leavenworth and Leavenworth County are named for him. The United States Penitentiary at Leavenworth and Henry Leavenworth Elementary School also bear his name, and the Disciplinary Barracks was sometimes referred to as "Leavenworth."

Not only did we have memorable military figures in our background, but the city was also host to significant political figures—most notably, Abraham Lincoln in December 1859. He was not yet president, but he visited Leavenworth's Planters Hotel during the lead-up to his campaign for the 1860 presidential bid. Planters, a four-story brick building with one hundred guestrooms, was considered the most magnificent hotel between St. Louis and San Francisco, and Lincoln was its most distinguished guest. He stayed there December 3–7.

Leavenworth was the last stop in Lincoln's visit to northeast Kansas during a time when tensions were flaring because of slavery. Lincoln spoke to an overflowing audience in Stockton Hall on December 3, a bitterly cold night. He was persuaded to stay in town and speak at Planters on December 9 to an estimated crowd of 1,500 who stood in the street to listen. Standing on the front steps of the hotel, he urged his listeners not to resort to violence as John Brown had just done, but instead to use the ballot box to voice their opinions on whether slavery should extend to Kansas. One newspaperman observed this was the "largest mass meeting that ever assembled on Kansas soil, and the greatest address ever heard here."

Though the hotel caught fire and was torn down in the 1950s, a replica of the steps remains next to a historical marker outlining their significance.

* * * * *

And so it was that in Leavenworth, like thousands before me, I came to be, kicking and screaming, on March 24, 1937, at the old St. John's Hospital on the corner of Seventh and Kickapoo streets—the first hospital established by the Sisters of Charity of Leavenworth in 1867. I was christened Edward F. Reilly Jr., after my father, Edward F., and great-grandfather, Captain Edward F., who fought in the Battle of Wilson Creek for the Union. My birth must have been a big thing for my parents, Ed and Marian, and an even bigger news item for *The Leavenworth Times*, since my picture and birth announcement were featured on a prominent page.

Ed introduced Marian to our home on Broadway, one of the early ones in his business of developing homes. Mom said when he took her there, she looked out to see nothing but fields. She knew he was a dreamer when he started talking about the subdivision he was building starting with that home.

Marian Sullivan had her own dreams when they first met. She attended Saint Mary College, majored in theatre and voice, and was a magnificent soprano. After graduation and various performances, she met Ed, who was a musician in his own right. A superb violinist, he worked his way through the Kansas City Law School with his Ed Reilly Orchestra. When he heard my mother sing, he persuaded her to do several gigs with the orchestra for Shrine functions. This led to a courtship that certainly wasn't as long as my own, but it resulted in their marriage and ultimately to my birth.

The story I most remember was when he asked her out one night after one of their gigs. She thought it was for dinner, but instead it was for a five-cent Coke.

* * * * *

As the first and now oldest in the Reilly clan, I must have been a challenge, as my mother and father said I was always on the move. My early memories consisted of playing doctor with the neighborhood kids and the typical, "You show me yours and I'll show you mine," which led to my getting caught by my mother behind the bushes of our home checking out the next-door neighbor's daughter. I might add she was older and more experienced—but we both ended up paying dearly for this with the spanking of all time.

As kids, we were fortunate that our parents took us on nearly all their trips, and we discovered our parents had different preferences while traveling. While my mother often insisted we get to our destination efficiently, my dad loved to stop at every site along the way. "Let's stop and see the World's Largest Ball of Twine," or the biggest rattlesnake known to man, or the statue of Paul Bunyan, and so on. This is probably indicative of their differing views on life; as always, my dad was the dreamer.

My father always wanted to explore the Colorado mountains in a Lincoln automobile that gave us a lot of trouble. As the driver, I found myself in and out of the car playing with the throttle to get us over the mountain and back to civilization. That's a memory that never leaves you—looking down from Pikes Peak at the ground 3,000 to 4,000 feet below. I feel fortunate indeed. Other trips had more practical purposes but still offered chances for excitement. On a family trip to Mobile, Alabama, where Dad was building Reilly Homes, I got the chance to almost drown in the ocean while wading with my Uncle Ray Wolters and first cousin, Dr. Ray Wolters. Fortunately, the seal hole I stepped in was only four feet deep, and I was pulled out easily.

The family trips to Evergreen, Colorado, that we took from the time I was about three gave me a chance to breathe, since I had apparently developed asthma. When I was about seven, an attack almost did me in. My parents finally discovered a quick shot of adrenaline from Dr. Bennet's nurse, Sally, was enough to get me going after an attack. The lack of air-conditioning sometimes seemed to trigger attacks; in those days, when it was hot, the only place for air-conditioned comfort was the Hollywood Theater on Fifth and Delaware streets, which later became the Performing Arts Theater. The building, now one of the few remaining art deco theaters left in the state, was placed on the Kansas Register of Historic Places in 1985 and on the National Register two years later.

Growing up in a city the size of Leavenworth was a great privilege, since we knew so many families, and they tended to look after one another and watch after the children. They were never bashful about telling your parents if you misbehaved. This allowed us to do things as kids we may not have done had we not felt part of a close community.

Mary Ann, my sister, reminds me of a great number of stunts we pulled since we were so close in age. Once, Mary Ann and I laid a dummy in the middle of Broadway, causing drivers to panic. My brother Jerry, who was younger, tended to be the innocent one, but he was pulled into the action as he matured. Bill Lyons, who grew up behind us, was a great friend, and we tended to keep the neighborhood in motion.

Out of my many misdeeds, I can now safely confess we were guilty of only a few true indiscretions. One I remember well was when we were lighting fireworks, and we accidentally set fire to the evergreens and other trees behind Bud and Trick Hinz's home on Columbia Street. There was also a rock-throwing incident at the Oliver house—our rock missed the main door and went through the glass storm door instead. We got caught for this, and we paid. We really didn't turn over Mrs. Hardeman's birdbath, though. The Reilly dog, a Saint Bernard named Mike, was just trying to get a drink, but nobody believed we were innocent.

And then there was the Polish Park Pavilion, just a block away on Broadway, that served as the hideaway for a lot of neighbor kids. There was always some kind of party going on there. Officials didn't know about the trap door inside the floor of the hall that allowed access inside. Wow, what parties we had—nothing illegal, but definitely memorable. Either way, the statute of limitations has passed, I'm pretty sure.

As I got older, I remember wanting to learn how to hunt and fish. It was great guys like Dewey Miller, Bringer Miller, Slim Hall, Jim Studdard, Dr. Donald Snow, and others who introduced me to those activities. They took me under their wing and taught me all I know about gun safety and how to catch the big ones. I remember their famous hunt and fishing club across the Missouri River on Mud Lake. I shot my first duck in their presence, and they assigned me to clean it.

As I got older, they let me accompany them to more serious trips to Huron, South Dakota, with the pheasant hunting pros—Dr. Snow, Bert Collard, George Bernhardt, and Perry Black. We would wake up to find the haystacks covered with cock and hen pheasants just waiting for us, but only until we stepped outside. Then try to find them! One vivid memory of my first trip to Huron and Hurdlicka's farm was the Hurdlicka brothers putting me between them in their pickup truck with a shotgun. My mission was to shoot across them and hit a jackrabbit as they raced across the fields at forty miles an hour. They claimed this was to determine whether I could shoot prior to the pheasant hunt. Frankly, I thought I might get killed that evening, just being in that pickup and jumping every rut, ravine and creek bed. So much for the big-game hunter—but we did get our limit of birds, and no one got shot.

In those days, we could go target-practicing on the Missouri River. I remember Ronnie Bacon taking me down on the Second Street Bridge when I was fourteen and throwing targets like bottles and cans in the water to see if I could shoot them with my .22 rifle. One item that looked like a plastic bottle floated by, and I zeroed in on it. I got it, only to have him tell me it was a condom. In those days, Leavenworth had no sewage plant, so we prided ourselves on sending Leavenworth mementoes to Kansas City via the Missouri River.

Fishing with Slim Hall was always a challenge, as he knew where the fish were in any body of water in Kansas. Slim sold us our first inboard/outboard boat, which we docked on the Yllier Lake built in the 1970s. We have fond memories of our mother telling everyone that the hole in the ground would fill in six months. She was right and through prayer proved it. It was the beginning of advancing our water-skiing techniques and teaching my nephews and nieces—JR, Mike, and Kathleen—as well as a host of other weekend guests.

* * * * *

Besides all the fun and games of youth, there were plenty of lessons learned; experiences can teach us a great deal if we're paying attention. One experience, which I still remember vividly, taught me and my friend Lou Klemp an important lesson when we were probably fifteen or sixteen years old.

My dad was a lawyer but also a wise businessman who invested in real estate when he had a few extra bucks. I remember some of the small homes he purchased in those early days of the late thirties and forties that he rented to those who couldn't afford to buy a home. I was often charged with collecting the rents each month or hounding some poor soul who was sixty days in arrears. After a day of collecting, Lou and I decided to visit the carnival that had just come to town, located on an empty lot behind Saint Mary College.

Unfortunately, we fell into the trap of a game where you place a bet and hope to win double your wager—or maybe a teddy bear—by rolling balls into various holes. How stupid we could be! I quickly lost the more than $1,100 I'd collected in rent money. When we realized what we'd done, we were devastated and began hatching a plan to recover the funds. As luck would have it, the vehicle I was driving overheated, and we headed for home—only to be met by my Irish mother. She quickly surmised, based on how we looked, that something had happened, and she demanded to know where we'd been.

"The carnival," Lou admitted, and my heart sank, as I knew what the next words out of her mouth would be—"What happened?" I had to confess we'd lost all the rent money Dad had sent me to collect.

"Get in the car," she ordered, after she picked up her trusty ball bat. "We're going to the sheriff's office and then the carnival." She wasn't fooling, and off we went, both of us in a panic about what would happen next. After Mom explained to the sheriff what had transpired, he decided it was in his best interest to go to the carnival too, to ensure she didn't get arrested. That wouldn't have looked good with Dad in the mayor's office.

As we walked the gangway to the tent where we'd been only an hour before, I grew even more nervous. When the operator saw us, he turned his back, but then he heard the sound of the bat hitting his counter. The first words out of his mouth were, "I've never seen these guys!"

The sheriff quickly contradicted him, explaining we'd been there an hour prior and had lost a lot of money. The operator insisted he didn't know us, but the sheriff replied, "You'd better rethink that because Mrs. Reilly is prepared to tear down every tent, and you've only been open one day."

"How much did they say they lost?" he demanded. I responded, "Eleven hundred dollars," and he finally suggested, "How about $500 and a teddy bear?" Well, the bat pounded on the counter again, and the sheriff informed him the mayor's wife was prepared to close down the carnival, and he would not be interfering. Finally, the furious operator pulled out the roll of bucks he'd collected and shelled out the $1,100. None of us will ever forget the lesson learned, and the mayor was never informed of what transpired.

We were forbidden to go back to the carnival, which moved on. That charge not to gamble lasted most of my life, until a trip to Las Vegas where I was intelligent enough to realize you can't beat a man at his own game. The best policy is to stay away from temptation in the first place.

*****

Bill Lyons, my neighbor and classmate through grade school and high school, followed politics over the years and was once a county official. During our school days, he and I often drove to his grandparents' farm in Kickapoo to hunt or hike. One evening, both of us, who were born just days apart, decided to take a ride out Highway 5 near the state women's prison—the place we all knew once had a tunnel of love to the men's prison.

A few miles past the prison, we saw two women walking alone on the highway. Being the gentlemen we were, we were concerned for their welfare and asked if they needed a ride. They climbed into the back of my Mercury pretty quickly, and we hadn't gone more than a few more miles when the red cherry lights started flashing behind my car—yes, I was driving.

The sheriff's deputies pulled us over, approached politely, and asked, "Did you pick up these ladies on the road?"

"Yes sir," was my equally polite and immediate response.

"Well, they're both walk-away prisoners from the prison," the deputy announced. "Ladies, please exit the car." They were promptly loaded in the patrol car and returned to what was then their home. As for Bill and me, it was another exciting time in our lives and one that thankfully didn't make the press.

So many events happened in Leavenworth in my era that trying to recall each one in which I had some involvement sometimes doesn't even sound real. But it's all true. This is one of them, a story few know that involved the Leavenworth penitentiary.

My father and Leavenworth attorney Homer Davis were good friends and had great respect for one another. The Davis family, with their eight children, were well known in the community. One son, Bob, a good friend of mine, became what his father had always dreamed for him: chief justice of the Kansas Supreme Court. Homer was a well-known attorney, and he had connections all over the country. One of these resulted in a call from the Las Vegas syndicate about an urgent need to go to USP (the penitentiary in Leavenworth) to pick up Benny Binion, who was being released. Like many incarcerated there, his background indicated crimes much more serious than tax evasion, but that's why he was there. Apparently, there was a detainer on him, and the US Marshals planned to pick him up.

As the story goes, Homer called my father to ask if he would accompany him to the penitentiary to ensure Benny was picked up before law enforcement arrived. He was to be delivered to the Kansas City airport to catch a flight to Vegas, where gambling was legal. I was to learn later from Dad that Benny had been making Las Vegas history since the 1950s, when the Texas gambler introduced the Horseshoe Club. This was the first real gambling hall and saloon in Vegas, and it was known as the place to go for high rollers' action and generous comps for his players. He went on to own The Mint Hotel and doubled his ownership in Las Vegas downtown property. He was passionate about giving his players excitement, good odds, and superb service, or as his motto goes: "Good food cheap. Good whiskey cheap. And a good gamble."

After the dust settled, I learned my father and Homer were Benny's guests in Vegas. I had the pleasure in my teens of visiting the Flamingo Hotel on the Strip with my parents, and the first place Dad wanted me to see was the famous Horseshoe Club.

* * * * *

Perhaps I've gone on a bit too long about these childhood memories. But what we get to experience in these early years has great bearing on how we move forward, how we make decisions, and how we deal with risk and accountability. Who we are or want to be is determined by the things we do, and what we do, in turn, determines who we are to ourselves and others. Mine was a small-town experience with quite a diverse set of communities—the Jewish community, the Catholic community, the

Protestant community—with which we got to engage. We all got along, and we had tremendous neighborhood parties because we didn't have TVs and other electronic gadgets, so it was a whole other world. As a result, we formed some tight bonds with each other that lasted well into our adult years.

Leavenworth had a large Jewish community, and we had one of the biggest synagogues in Missouri and Kansas. The Temple B'Nai Jeshurun, located at Sixth and Osage streets, was the first Jewish place of worship in Kansas, built in 1866 because a large Jewish community established residence in Leavenworth. The original frame building was razed in 1916 and replaced by the present structure, which served as a place of worship for Leavenworth's Jewish congregation until the 1970s. A plaque was placed at the site in 2012 by the Leavenworth County Historical Society and the Jewish American Society for Historic Preservation. After it was no longer used for worship, it was sold and converted to apartments.

That community got smaller because many Jewish businesses moved to Kansas City. My father, who had attended the old Kansas City School of Law with Harry Truman, knew most all the merchants because, when they started the insurance business, his father wrote policies for most of the Jewish merchants in Leavenworth. I think my father bought my mother's ring from one of the Jewish merchants.

I followed a similar path, as I bought a diamond from Paul Hess, a runaway Kansas Senate colleague, which I put in my wife's ring for our wedding. Hess, elected as a state representative in 1970, served in the Senate from 1972–1984. He represented Wichita for 12 years before moving to Overland Park and losing an election bid in 1984. Once the chairman of the powerful Kansas Senate Committee on Ways and Means, Hess fled the United States with his three small sons after he was charged with felony theft in Johnson County. He pled guilty to stealing a client's insurance settlement. He was charged in a federal fugitive warrant after he traveled to the Middle East with his three young sons. His estranged wife told reporters Egyptian authorities helped her gain custody of the children after Hess was found in Cairo, Egypt. The

FBI began searching for him because he was charged with illegal flight to avoid prosecution.

At some point after he'd served federal time, Hess met with me and showed me a bag of diamonds. He'd moved to California and was marketing diamonds, working with jewelers who got their diamonds from Israel, one of the largest exporters. He threw the diamonds on my desk, and they were gorgeous. I asked if they were real and he said I could get them tested, which I did. Ultimately, I picked the largest diamond and put it in Luci's ring.

* * * * *

Of course, besides all the wonderful life education I got to call "childhood," there was my formal education as well. I started kindergarten at the Franklin School on Pennsylvania Avenue, which no longer exists. Later I went to Third Avenue School, and then it was off to Sacred Heart on Second Avenue. From then on, I went all through Catholic schools until high school, so I knew a lot of the nuns. It was a wonderful experience to grow up in, and it provided a fabulous education, but the nuns weren't afraid to use rulers on your palm, your hands, and your knuckles.

During my time in parochial school, I didn't receive the same exposure and life experiences that my peers outside of private schools did. This contributed to my decision to leave private schooling for public school. I wanted to broaden my horizons because, even at an early age, I realized the importance of living outside my comfort zone and experiencing the world as thoroughly as possible. I was set on attending Leavenworth High School also because they had an excellent Army Reserve Officers Training Corps (ROTC) program, which my father had completed when he attended the school. It was my desire to follow my father's footsteps not only through public school, but also through the ROTC program.

When he was in school, there wasn't such a push among the parishes to try to force you to go to the Catholic high school. But our local monsignor and pastor, Monsignor Selting at Sacred Heart Parish, did everything in his power to influence my parents to send me to the Catholic high school. Though my parents wished I had completed my Catholic education, I could not be dissuaded, and they respected my decision.

You can imagine that lunging from the security of a small Catholic grade school to a much larger public high school was a big step. However, since my father had done it, I was convinced I could too. I seemed to fit right in, making friends quickly with the kids who had come from St. Paul Lutheran School, with Jewish children, and with many international and military kids whose parents were associated with Fort Leavenworth. I made it through in four years, graduating with the Leavenworth High School Class of 1956, even though Howard Tolle, principal at the time, never thought that Robert Doran and I would make it.

Leavenworth High School required all boys to complete one year of ROTC training, but I decided to stay in the program for three years. Participating in ROTC had a profound and lasting impact on me. Even now, I think it was one of the greatest decisions I ever made. I entered the program as a boy and during the next three years, I was molded into a man and a leader. In ROTC, we learned traditional military skills like navigation and weapon handling, and we also completed various physical and drill exercises to ensure we were in good condition. While these skills were useful and would have been necessary for a military career, the hard work we put in, both inside and outside of school hours, instilled the values of hard work, teamwork, and dedication. And these were more valuable than being able to read a map or take apart an M1 .30 caliber rifle blindfolded.

The FBI recruited me out of high school with the expectation that I would attend school in Kansas City as I worked for them. While I'm sure my ROTC training and my interest in criminal justice would have served me well in the FBI, I decided to attend the University of Kansas in Lawrence.

Interestingly enough, one of the most difficult decisions I had to make upon entering KU in 1956 was which fraternity to pledge. I went through what was then called "Rush Week" on most campuses. Guys were running from fraternity house to fraternity house to see who would select them. It was quite an experience, and there were moments when this kid from Leavenworth said, "Why am I doing this?" At the end of rush, I had bids from three houses, so I had to make a decision. I called—guess who—my dad, and he drove over to tell me I had to make a decision quickly. He told me they don't fool around when it comes to offering and withdrawing an offer. At least, that was the case in 1956.

As a lad coming from Leavenworth High School to the big university, I thought being in a frat house would give me more support than KU college housing. I ended up pledging Sigma Alpha Epsilon fraternity, and I've never regretted it. This great group of guys supported and looked after one another. We studied together, worked together, and sometimes even chased the same girls, but we were always brothers in the bonds. The relationships that developed are never forgotten. I encourage all men, including my son Joseph, to consider a fraternity when entering college. I loved the experiences I had, and I believed that given my son's personality, he would too. And he did. Joe pledged Alpha Gamma Rho at the University of Maryland, and I am sure it will have a positive impact on his life.

There is no question that my membership in Sigma Alpha Epsilon, which stressed the concept of service as a mark of good character, has been one of the cornerstones in my life. The emphasis on causes that support the greater good was another factor in my volunteering and giving time and energy toward a worthy cause. The pledge we memorized and repeated often, "The True Gentleman," tells it all:

> The true gentleman is the man whose conduct proceeds from good will and an acute sense of propriety, and whose self-control is equal to all emergencies; who does not make the poor man conscious of his poverty, the obscure man of his obscurity, or any man of his inferiority or deformity; who is himself humbled if necessity compels him to humble another; who does not flatter wealth, cringe before power, or boast of his own possessions or achievements; who speaks with frankness but always

with sincerity and sympathy; whose deed follows his word; who thinks of the rights and feelings of others, rather than his own; and who appears well in any company, a man with whom honor is sacred and virtue safe.
– John Walter Wayland

That pledge has been one of the roadmaps in my life, guiding me through the years.

The KU days were wonderful, and some excellent professors helped me through some tough subjects and provided wise counseling. I wasn't the best student, but I persisted, and I graduated in 1960. The subject that helped most was Army ROTC, which I continued from Leavenworth High, and where I had risen to the rank of major in the cadet corps. At KU it was the guys from Leavenworth High who could read the maps and tear down an M1 rifle and put it back together at night. We had it when it came to beating anyone else in the class, and our grades said so. I have no doubt this experience greatly impacted my desire to serve and aided in the development of the leadership skills that would become necessary later. Leaders are not born; leaders are developed through experience, wisdom, and a lot of mentoring. ROTC provided me with all of this.

My time in ROTC further instilled the value of service, and because of this, I believe everyone should serve in some way for at least a year. It may not necessarily be in the military, but the impact service can have is invaluable. I am convinced that my style of leadership based on service became my hallmark in the Kansas Legislature, and it was fostered during my time in ROTC.

In November 2007, KU inducted me into their Hall of Fame. I was proud I could take my son to that ceremony on the same day we attended KU's Homecoming with his Uncle Jerry and his wife Charla, and Aunt Mary Ann. One thing is for sure, having my son with me to experience these moments is among the highlights of my life. Of course, sitting next to "Wilt the Stilt" Chamberlain in Professor Kollmorgen's geography class is a close second. We both passed the class, but I often wondered if Wilt knew where he was going in his life. His photo hangs in our home from 1959, when he visited the Guardian Angel Orphanage in Leavenworth.

Toward the end of my college career, I discovered I couldn't pass the medical examinations to officially join the Army because of my history of asthma as a child. When I was about nine or ten, I had an asthma attack at summer camp, which was in my medical record. Though it never happened again, it disqualified me from serving in the Army. My father even tried to get a waiver for me since he was friendly with some generals, but no such luck. I was extremely disappointed I couldn't continue my military training and start a career with the Army. The draft was in effect at the time, and I wanted to enter as a second lieutenant rather than be drafted, but because of my childhood medical records, I could do neither.

* * * * *

During my days at KU, I didn't think a lot about politics. Initially, I wanted to major in business, inspired by my family's business where I had worked since I was a kid. However, my advisor, Dr. Francis Heller, as politely as he could, suggested I consider another major, not only because of my poor performance in my business classes but also because of my growing political interests. Was he ever right! I won't say I sailed through college after that, but it was certainly more fun and something I could relate to, and something I worked hard to complete.

I began looking at political science and settled on that major in my second year. I got involved in Young Republican activities with a student I knew, Tom Van Sickle, who later served in the Legislature when I did. We became good friends. He encouraged me to become more seriously involved, and I ended up as the Young Republican National Committeeman in the Republican collegiate group. I put the degree to work in 1963, three years after graduation, when I ran for the Kansas House. What I learned in college served me well.

Since I was unable to join the Army from ROTC, when I graduated from KU in 1960 I decided to return home and continue working at my family's business. My father and grandfather started the Ed Reilly

Agency in 1925, which specialized in real estate and insurance. My father was an attorney who graduated from the old Kansas City School of Law, working his way through school with the Ed Reilly Orchestra, and my grandfather was involved in county level politics. When my grandfather, H. V. Reilly, was defeated in his bid for reelection as county treasurer, the two of them decided to establish a business in the community. Even so, in the 1950s, my father followed in H. V.'s footsteps and got involved in politics as well.

He quickly learned that entering public service wanting to accomplish something good doesn't shield you from those who want to defeat you, either because they want your job, or they want someone else to have it. My father wanted to serve on the Water Board. Opponents claimed he only wanted to serve to get a line run to his farm. This wasn't true, but it cost him the election. If people can't find something to hold against you, they will make it up. But later, my father ran for mayor and was elected by a large margin.

He was elected without opposition during his first term, the first mayoral candidate without opposition in one hundred years, according to *The Leavenworth Times*. He served two terms. At the time, the mayor of Leavenworth was sort of a king. He had control of the police and fire departments and presided over all city commission meetings. At this time, the state attorney general considered Leavenworth to be open to a lot of things such as illegal gambling. Liquor also flowed freely, which appealed to the soldiers at Fort Leavenworth. I fondly recollect my father firing the chief of police because of one club, the Uniform Rank Club, which also had girls available. The position of city manager hadn't been created yet and wouldn't have been accepted in Leavenworth at that time, so during my father's tenure, the mayor was a powerful person in the city. Because of that, my father didn't pursue his legal career. Instead, he and my grandfather went on to build one of the most successful realty and insurance firms in eastern Kansas, a legacy I was proud to be part of.

Later my father and one of his friends started a bank in Lansing, the largest small town in Kansas without a bank. They had previously had one, but it had gone under due to some malfeasance. We were not bankers, by any means, but we were interested in providing the service for the community. We were fortunate that, for the most part, we were able to hire competent operators. So there it was: The First State Bank of Lansing. I ultimately served as vice president at the bank. Before you go thinking this was some glamorous corner office job, it wasn't. Although I would sit in on the meetings, my tasks were often more "people-centric." I would go out occasionally, when necessary, to check the local farmer using his cattle as collateral, to make sure the cattle were there. I checked to see if people were doing what they said they were doing, and so on. But it was a good experience.

However, once the bank was robbed at gunpoint on June 30, 1970, it proved time to exit the banking business. That came to pass in the summer of 1972, when I attended the Republican National Convention to nominate Richard Nixon. I met a farmer's wife there, Mary Alice Lair, and her husband was looking for another bank for one of his sons. So it happened—another opportunity in life to move on and focus on the business we knew.

At the realty and insurance agency, I delivered the yearly calendar and yearbooks to clientele. Because of that, I got to know the community well. These business contacts and personal relationships I built came in handy when I began my political career representing my community. I always felt like I was engaged in advising on insurance or real estate matters, but it became obvious political advice was also possible. When I decided to be the next Reilly to go into public service, I called on many of these people personally and asked for their support. I asked if they'd hang my political posters in their business—and many did.

Being involved in insurance and real estate proved valuable, and sometimes I got some education I didn't get at the University of Kansas. I was often charged with measuring and photographing buildings to be insured. One such experience led me to the second floor of a business where I learned why mirrors were so important. The room I stumbled on used the ones on the ceiling and side walls to highlight the different positions in the art of making love. Overwhelmed, I excused myself, only to keep rolling the automatic tape measure I had. I learned a great deal that day, including what a real orgasm was all about. I still wonder what happened to that understanding couple who weren't stopping for any reason.

The Reillys have been one of the most prominent Catholic families in Kansas, even during times when it wasn't easy to be a Roman Catholic. I consider being born and raised in the Leavenworth community a great privilege. Entering the family business in my hometown was one of the smartest moves I could have made. I credit that experience, along with my social upbringing, for making it possible for me to meet so many clients and make new friends along the way, some of whom would eventually catapult me into the career of public service.

Our past sometimes makes its own plans for us. My great-great-grandfather immigrated to the United States from Ireland as a teenager and enlisted in the Union Army. He fought at the battle of Wilson Creek in that hot August of 1861. My grandfather served several decades in county government, and my father served as unopposed mayor of Leavenworth for the first of his two terms.

So the idea of public service wasn't foreign to my family. Perhaps for me too it had always been not a matter of "if" but "when."

The Reilly name is well known in Ireland with most residents found in Counties Cavan, Longford, Meath, Fermanagh and Monaghan. In the Reilly coat of arms, the bloody hand symbolizes Faith, Sincerity, and Justice. The motto of the family is "With Fortitude and Prudence."

I endured disappointments with fortitude and patience when I persevered in seeking the post of Irish ambassador, then the appointment as chairman of the United States Parole Commission, and finally the nomination as United States Observer to the International Fund for Ireland. The latter nomination extended my opportunity to serve the homeland by working for the extension of a lasting peace.

As for the other segment of our motto, prudence is defined as "the ability to govern and discipline oneself by the use of reason." I'm not sure I fit *Merriam-Webster's* second definition of "sagacity or shrewdness," but

I believe that "skill and good judgment in the use of resources" is fitting. As for "caution or circumspection as to danger or risk," I can only be grateful in view of the decisions made as a public servant that I have survived all these years.

I became a member of the Ancient Order of Hibernians, which evolved in the 1600s from the need to protect priests from possible death in Ireland because they practiced their faith. It was founded in the United States in New York in May 1836 with the mission and motto of promoting Irish culture, friendship, unity, and Christian charity. Councils exist all over the United States and make a real impact with their charitable work and the promotion of Irish culture through parades and other celebrations.

2

Entering the Public Square

When my father was young, the Ku Klux Klan burned a cross in the front yard of his parents' home. His father was an official in the county government at the time and was expected to seek reelection as county treasurer. I guess this was their way of sending a message to a local Catholic politician.

This would have been in the 1920s; I never heard an exact date, but since my father and grandfather started their business in 1925, it probably was sometime around the 1924 election. In the 1920s, the KKK had a resurgence in Kansas, with as many as 100,000 members at one point. Billing themselves as ultrapatriotic and aiming to keep America American, the Ku Klux Klan targeted several groups, including Catholics, black people, Jews, and immigrants.

Ramon Powers, former director of the Kansas Historical Society, found that H. V. Reilly and wife "transferred property to the 'Colored Methodist Episcopal Church' in January of 1921," according to the January 16, 1921, edition of the *Leavenworth Post*. There was no mention of any cross burning in the newspaper, but Powers speculates the transaction could have triggered a response from the KKK.

Powers added that the *Leavenworth Post*, on November 6, 1922, said the KKK "has not established itself in Leavenworth, notwithstanding some of the candidates have been charged with affiliating." That's what I believe happened to my grandfather—the Klan endorsed a popular man in town who defeated him.

But Leavenworth was soon to organize a Klan organization. According to the December 30, 1923, edition of the *Kansas City Star*, "The Leavenworth Ku Klux Klan made its first public appearance with a parade of fifteen motor cars down the main street at 10:30 o'clock tonight (December 29). Two of the cars carried fiery crosses."

The August 21, 1924, edition of the *Kansas City Star* provides some details of the Klan's organizing in the community. It notes that on July 10, 1923, "a band of men" met outside town and signed the Leavenworth charter petition to become members of the Knights of the Ku Klux Klan: "Last Tuesday night, just thirteen months and sixteen days later, the Leavenworth Provisional Klan with its twenty-five hundred members met and received the charter which made it a full-fledged organization, with its own officers and with the privilege of functioning as any other organization." According to this article, "Leavenworth Klan is one of the last Klans in the state to be organized. The delivery of the charter makes it one of the strongest Klans in the state. Leavenworth has been known previously as the town in which a Klan could not be organized."

Once it organized, the group was not hesitant to appear publicly. The Kansas State Historical Society website has a photo that demonstrates this; on the back, it is described as an image of a "Ku Klux Klan funeral at the Baptist Church located on the southwest corner of Sixth and Seneca streets." It is dated only as sometime between 1920–1929. Clearly visible in the photo are congregants wearing white pointed hoods and robes entering the church.

"Sending a message" is a favorite activity of groups of this sort. It may not be burning a cross, but things like this are still happening today. So when I told my father I planned to run for a seat in the Kansas house, he didn't encourage me. He was concerned that some of the elements of the Klan still existed in the community—not the individuals involved in the incident when he was a youth, but perhaps their children and grandchildren who might carry traces of feelings and stories passed from their elders.

What if they just said they're not going to support a Catholic running for office? We'd gone through all this with John F. Kennedy. The prediction was, "Nobody will vote for Kennedy; he's a Catholic." Well, thank God we got over that. I even voted for Kennedy (in 1960, the first presidential election I ever voted in) because I wanted to prove that you could elect somebody to office despite their religious affiliation—even though I was a Republican, and he was a Democrat.

My dad didn't think, initially, that I could get elected. Besides, at that time the Reilly Company was a small agency that relied on its full contingent of four employees. I'm sure he was thinking I'd be going to Topeka, and this would leave him holding down the fort with only a couple of other folks.

I'm sure both my parents wanted to protect me from disappointment. My mother eventually came around, but my father worried I wouldn't have a shot at winning the appointment. I can understand their concerns—especially from my dad, who had gone through that horrible experience in his youth. But I wasn't going to let that event impact my decision to run.

The opportunity came a short while after I had returned from college with my political science degree, when word got out that the Kansas House member, Robert Behee, was resigning from the post he'd held since 1961. His resignation stemmed from a controversy involving a dispute with a labor union. Suddenly there was a vacant House seat, and the Leavenworth County Republican Precinct Committee was in charge of selecting someone to fill the rest of that term.

A few years later, I was asked as a state senator to assist the Behee family who wished to have the bodies of some of their family, the Luherings, extricated from Mexico after a tragic accident. A drunk driver had crashed into the Luhering family, killing a number of them. Working with the Kansas congressional delegation, we were able to bring them home for burial. It wasn't easy then, and I'm sure it would be much more much more difficult now in view of our relationship with Mexico. That country generally wants extra payment for any service performed.

I was a Republican, but I considered myself a fairly moderate Republican, not leaning either way in terms of being a strong liberal or a strong conservative. Those were the days when you could say you were a moderate and get away with it. Nobody would question you. You could go either way, depending on the legislation and your own thoughts and philosophy.

It wasn't going to be an easy race, since at twenty-six, I was the second-youngest person in Kansas to seek a legislative seat. With no previous experience holding office, I wasn't well known to the Republicans on the county precinct committee. To top it off, Representative Behee had endorsed the former county attorney, James Fussell, to fill the post he was vacating. So I wasn't the favorite by a long shot, as Jim Fussell had a head start and many commitments before I jumped in the race. But after consulting with our county chairman and state senator, John Murray, I took the challenge.

I had four to five weeks to campaign to win the votes of the committee precinct members and I gave it my all. I made it a point to call on all the men and women on the committee. In some cases, it was multiple times over the weeks to encourage them to support me and to share my views with them. Making myself and my positions known to them was integral to winning the seat. I ate more cookies and candy and drank more coffee during that period than is recommended by common sense. But people were nice. Sometimes they told me they weren't going to vote for me, and they'd still offer me cookies and drinks. They were honest. I don't know if that would happen today, but they were right up front with me—"Ed, we've already committed to Jim Fussell." "OK, I understand, but all I ask is that you just give me some consideration." And so on, until the last possible moment. I had a black book where I kept track of who they said they supported. It was a bleak picture going into the decisive meeting the night of the assembly. But with everyone I'd met, I insisted I was interested in going to Topeka and fulfilling the mission of representing Leavenworth.

Unfortunately, my father didn't have much advice for me since he had run unopposed. He had it easy. He told me he'd never had an enemy until he entered politics, and he didn't want me to have to face that. But my parents eventually supported me once they saw I was serious about winning the seat. My father even visited Wyandotte County on my behalf to meet with a political leader there, Sheriff Red Edwards. Edwards was known to have a great deal of clout in the Wyandotte County community, which was primarily Democratic, and his support would help immensely. Parts of Wyandotte County were in the House district then.

On the night of the selection at the Leavenworth County Courthouse, my father was in tears, telling me I should be prepared to lose and not to hold any hard feelings. He reminded me of his father's experience when he was defeated for county treasurer after many years of devoted service. I must say I was prepared for a loss. But I went with a positive attitude and a desire to persuade those precinct men and women that I could do the job given the opportunity. Each candidate had a maximum of ten minutes to present his case.

My opponent was a qualified gentleman who was a former county attorney. Quite well-known and bright, James Fussell was in his late forties or fifties. I think he was as shocked as I was that a twenty-six-year-old was running against him. But we were cordial to each other to the bitter end.

Fussell spoke before me after winning the coin toss. Per the regulations, I had to wait in the hallway while he spoke. I had an idea of what Fussell would say in his speech about me: that I was too young and too inexperienced. However, I happened to run into an old high school classmate that night who was working in the courthouse. He confirmed my suspicions about Fussell's speech. Freddy Lambkins had been mopping the floors in the back of the courtroom before he came back into the hallway where I was waiting.

"You're right, Ed," he told me. Fussell came after me exactly how I expected. According to Freddy, he made four points: I was too young, I hadn't served before like he had, I had no experience in the Kansas Republican Party, and I lacked the knowledge needed to hold elected office because I'd never served. Going into the meeting, I knew if everyone who was already committed to my opponent stayed that way, I would lose by a wide margin. So after getting this information from my classmate, I was determined to respond to each of Fussell's critical remarks and to give them my ten-minute argument for why I should be elected over a much more experienced political figure.

The first thing I did was thank everybody for the wonderful experience I'd had visiting with them since they'd been so nice to me. I said I could imagine what my opponent said about me. That's not what I'd written, so I threw my three-by-five cards dramatically over my shoulder. I said, "You know, I realize I'm probably stepping out as a neophyte here to run for an office when I haven't served the party very well or very long. Even though I've been a Republican, I haven't served the party. I've not been doing some of the things that you folks have or that Mr. Fussell has. But I'm also taking the position that those of us who are coming along have to be given a chance to show what we can do. You really can't know until you've given a person the opportunity to gain that experience."

They called for the vote, which was all secret ballot. The result was two to one. I've never forgotten that. Talk about being shocked and surprised! I remember Mr. Fussell standing up and politely requesting a recount right away. They did it immediately, and the results were still sixty out of eighty votes for me. I realized a lot of people either weren't shooting straight when they said who they supported, or they really made a big change in their position.

When I called home with the results, my mother said my dad had gone to bed crying, armed with a glass of scotch. Mother had been praying to the Blessed Virgin and lighting candles faithfully. I really believe she thought we would succeed. She was the eternal optimist throughout my career and her life. She always supported me—and so did Dad—if I wanted to try to do something. I said, "Well, wake him up and pour me a glass. We won, and I'm coming home as Representative Ed."

To say my life changed at that point would be an understatement. I was cast into a whole new exciting life with people from throughout Kansas. After Governor John Anderson signed my papers, I arrived at the State House in January 1963. Though I was still recouping from the surprise of my victory, I was ready to learn all I could and to put my political science degree to work for Kansas. Representative John Gardner was assigned by the Speaker of the House to look after me and introduce me to House procedure. He made it clear early on: "The House procedure for you, Reilly, will be to escort all the people to the Dome who are here as guests of the Legislature." Well, that was my assignment. Perhaps not what I was expecting, but I did it faithfully. And that's probably why I have knee problems today.

My Kansas House tenure was short, but it was a great training ground for the next challenge. The Legislature was to redistrict, and Leavenworth County was going to lose one of its two House seats. This meant if I ran for the remaining seat, I would face a senior representative who had served many years, most of them without opposition. Ambrose Dempsey was well liked in general and really loved by those who knew and served with him. He was the epitome of the Irish Democrat—never met a stranger, attended every wake and funeral service, and knew every farmer in Leavenworth County. The Dempsey family was one of the biggest and best-known Irish Catholic families in Leavenworth County, all bachelors. The ball was in his court. I had to decide, with only one House seat for our county, to run against Ambrose or try for the Kansas Senate . . . the Kansas Senate?!

Now my parents really thought I'd stepped off a cliff. How could I be considering the Senate when I'd just entered the House? As luck would have it, our senator, John Murray, also a close friend, was giving serious consideration to running for the United States Second District congressional seat. When he decided to run against Chester Mize for the Republican nomination, I immediately jumped in to run for the Kansas Senate. Prior to doing that, I approached Representative Dempsey, as a courtesy, to inquire about his intent. After numerous meetings, he indicated he wasn't sure what he was going to do. It was then my father got in the arena with me and told me, "Call the shots. Go to the courthouse and file for the Senate. Don't wait. He's not going to tell you; he's just playing a guessing game. Son, go for the Senate. I've always wanted to know a senator." I think that was the day before the filing deadline, and I went to the courthouse and declared, "I'm filing for the Senate!"

My opponent Arthur Hanson, a nice gentleman from Wyandotte County, was quick to point out I was the second youngest member in the Legislature, and the slogan on all his signs was: "Don't elect a boy to do a man's work." Where had I heard that before? Talk about being put down and made to question your abilities. It caused me to pause and reflect, but I plowed on, and thanks to the support of family and friends, I was once again successful. I won a four-year Senate term by a two-to-one margin. It was the beginning of a career of commitment to serve others and to do what I could to repay those who had helped me in business and public service.

The election watch for my first Senate election was an event to remember. We picked the Colonial Kitchen at Third and Cherokee for the watch party, and campaign managers Rick and Larry Schneider and all our volunteers gathered for the vote count. It dragged on late, and we took over the kitchen after the restaurant closed, frying bacon and eggs until late the next morning when the results were finalized. It was all a hand count in those days, and precincts were often slow in getting the votes to the county clerk.

As I arrived in the Senate, once again as one of the younger members, all eyes were cast on this neophyte, curiously questioning, "What do we have here?" Serving in the Senate, whether it's state or national, is more challenging than serving in the House. Senators believe in showing their individual personalities, and they expect senatorial courtesy and decorum. I learned this quickly, thanks to good friends and a class of twenty-four, all of whom entered as new senators. It was a great group of ladies and gentlemen who respected each other. I learned four Sigma Alpha Epsilon fraternity brothers, of various ages, also served in the Senate. This helped me, as they were quick to advise and counsel. I also reunited with my good friend Tom Van Sickle, who had encouraged me to pursue public service back at KU. He was chairman, and I was committeeman, for the college Republican group. Tom also happened to be the youngest senator, and I was the second youngest.

My first four years in the Senate were exciting, and I learned the ropes quickly. I felt comfortable, and as I gained more knowledge about state government, I became confident I was in the right place. Since I was still a bachelor during those years, I courted many ladies—some from Kansas, others from around the United States, and a number from Ireland. I often visited Ireland, as it was one of my favorite countries and the home of my ancestors. And that is an education in itself for a twenty-seven-year-old man from Leavenworth, Kansas.

Some lessons I had to learn the hard way in those early days—even years—in the Senate. One involved a controversial fair housing bill. Senator George Haley, one of the first African American legislators in Kansas, was pushing the anti-discrimination bill. The brother of Alex Haley, the Pulitzer-Prize winning author of *Roots*, George faced more than his share of discrimination, especially when he attended the University of Arkansas law school. He endured much—he was spit at; feces were thrown at him—but he never gave up. He was definitely a man to remember for the courage and conviction he showed as a law school student, when he faced horrible abuse and humiliation. The article written about him in *Reader's Digest* is testimony to a great public servant. Both he and his son, David, now a Kansas senator, demonstrate that those with gumption, virtue, and fortitude can survive even in a world that often projects hate toward others.

I was privileged to speak at the funerals of both Senator Haley and his wife Doris, which were conducted in the DC area. I shall never forget him, what he represented, and what he and his brother Alex Haley, the revered author, brought to the public square.

At any rate, in that early time in the Senate, because of pressure from peers, as well as attorneys and realtors, I voted against that fair housing bill. My dad read about the bill in the newspaper, and when I returned home on a weekend, he asked how I'd voted on it. I told him I'd voted against it. "You what?" my father was incensed. "Why would you vote that way?" I started to explain about "some of my colleagues" but that wasn't enough for my father. "You didn't answer the question," he insisted. "What made you go down that road? You were never told to discriminate."

I stuttered and stammered some more about the pressure from realtors and lawyers, but I was humiliated and felt bad about it. Two or three days later, there was a move in the Senate to reconsider the bill, and as you can imagine, I switched my vote. I also approached Senator Haley, a Republican who was part of my class of senators. I apologized and shook hands with George and told him, "That's not the way I was brought up." I explained that my father had often lent money to minorities during his career and taught me not to discriminate.

"That's not the way I was brought up and educated," I reiterated. That was an important part of my life, and it took my father to bring it to my attention. It was definitely a lesson learned.

Still another lesson came when I voted on a highway bill. I had promised state Senator Ernie Strahan, a Salina Republican, that I would vote for it, but when it came to the floor, I voted no. I got a call from Senate President Paul Wunsch, an attorney from Kingman who ruled that body for sixteen years, beginning in 1945. "I need to talk to you in my office," Wunsch said.

I will never forget what he said. "I noticed you didn't vote for the bill," Wunsch observed, adding that he'd been assured there were enough votes to pass it and that I would vote for it. "You changed your vote," he said. "What was your reason?"

Again I tried the excuse of pressure from my colleagues. But he wasn't buying it either. "I have one word of advice for you," the veteran senator told me. "When you're bought, you stay bought." Though that might sound a bit negative, he went on to explain, "If you make a promise to vote for something you vote for it. You violated one of the codes in the Legislature that has to do with trust and integrity. You keep your promise."

Thankfully, this bill, too, was reconsidered, and I did vote for it. I guess you'd say I had to grow up and become a man—I had to become educated in how the process really worked.

My father was an important influence as I grew up, and I've recently been thinking about Dad and his energy and spirit during the time when we were at war and he was working his way through law school, riding the interurban electrified trolley from Leavenworth to Kansas City to earn that degree. All the while, his orchestra afforded him revenue to pay tuition and musicians. I also recall his keen interest in baseball, supporting the minor league Leavenworth Braves. I remember when I was a kid, he took me to a lot of their games at Wadsworth Park, later known as the Veterans' Park.

All this occurred during a tough period in America with the war and economy and President Franklin Roosevelt selling the New Deal. Not unlike today, you had to have the entrepreneurial spirit and a hell of a lot of guts to be a success. At the same time, his father was coming down with throat cancer after his defeat in county politics. And we think we have it rough? All this tells the story of a man who threw himself into the insurance business to help his father earn an income.

My father turned out to be a role model in another way, though it wasn't part of a legislative process. However, the experience reinforced the importance of keeping your word on things you'd committed to and trusting people.

It was the time Sam Walton and his son Rob came to Leavenworth looking for a site to establish Walmart Store #26. They didn't initially identify themselves or their plans, though. It was about 1970, and when the call came, I happened to be the only one in the office at Reilly & Sons. When I asked what the caller wanted, he said they wanted to look at commercial real estate.

I told him everyone else was gone, including our real estate manager, retired Colonel Dave Nunn. But the caller was not to be dissuaded. "Who are you?" he asked. I told him I was Ed Reilly and that I was also a state senator. "You're one of the principals of the firm, aren't you?" he asked. "We're at the Fort Leavenworth airport. Can you come and pick us up?"

I was familiar with the airport, since my father had negotiated the deal to use it during his tenure as mayor. So I picked up the man and his son, and I drove them to numerous commercial real estate sites. I took them to Twentieth and Spruce, to Fourth Street near Saint Mary's College, and several other spots. They expressed interest, but they still didn't tell me anything.

I must have spent close to two hours showing them the town and various properties, and it wasn't dark yet. "We have one other request," the older man said. "We want you to go up in our airplane with us."

That was a sore point. I told them my father always advised me to stick to commercial flights, not private two-engine planes.

"We want to see where the lights are," the man insisted. Their goal was to fly over the sites we'd just visited, looking for lights and homes. So I acquiesced and also mentioned future plans for a Twentieth Street freeway. The men said they'd get back to me.

Sure enough, they called the office two weeks later. At that point, we were referring all real estate calls to Colonel Nunn, and he, too, tried to find out what they had in mind for the Twentieth and Spruce site, but again they demurred. "Can we meet with you at the Kansas City airport?" the caller asked Nunn. "Why not?" I responded. I told my dad where we were going, and he wanted to come along.

When we walked into the airport, my dad took one look at the older man and said, "I know you."

"I know you, too," the man said when he looked at my dad. "Oh my God, they know one another," I said to Colonel Nunn. Dad recounted the time he and my mother went on vacation to Bentonville, Arkansas. Someone at their hotel mentioned a meeting that evening in the high school auditorium. They were curious and decided to check it out.

When they went inside the auditorium, they joined the rest of the crowd seated on those old-time plastic orange crates. There they heard Sam Walton, who owned a five-and-dime store in Bentonville, elaborate on his vision to provide stores nationwide that would reduce the cost of living so Walmart shoppers could live better. He spoke of warehouses across the country to distribute supplies to stores. Intrigued by his ideas, my father talked to Walton that night.

At the airport meeting, Walton announced his desire to build a store, along with a fifteen-thousand-foot pharmacy, at the Twentieth and Spruce site. We own that land, my father told him, and they shook hands. Dave Nunn started pressing the paperwork to complete the sale, but Walton motioned to my father. "The deal's done. We shook hands. We'll send you the paperwork signed."

That was it. Store #26, the first in Kansas, opened in early November 1970. It was a bold concept for Leavenworth, and a controversial move, since downtowns were wary of the impact a Walmart could have on their business. For me, though, it was another lesson from my father about meeting and trusting people. Trust and integrity were definitely uppermost for both men, and it's a lesson I took to heart.

Back to specific Senate experiences, though, I remember feeling that getting a woman's perspective on the issues we were grappling with was healthy and good for politics. As I recall, the first woman in the Senate while I was serving was Louise Porter, a rancher from Lyon County in western Kansas. Louise was a striking woman, and she had a real impact on the rest of us. We behaved better and listened to each other with more respect, among other things. Though Louise was the only woman in the Senate, in the House were Beatrice Jacquart from Santana, Harriet Graham from Wichita, and Dollie Newell from Stafford—all capable women who contributed a lot to the Kansas Legislature. At times, I believe a woman's temperament creates a more focused and direct environment when debating issues and looking for solutions.

There were many rigors of politics, and thanks to the people of Leavenworth, Jefferson, and Wyandotte counties who elected me for more than twenty-nine years to represent their interests, I was able to serve them in many functions. I was vice chairman of the Elections Committee; a member of the Congressional and Judicial Apportionment Committee; a member of the Arts, Cultural Resources Joint Committee; and chairman of the Federal and State Affairs Committee.

Luckily, we had an excellent support staff in the Research and Senate staff who provided the expertise necessary to make judgments in the best interests of our state. I also had my beautiful, personable sister Mary Ann by my side on the Senate floor as my secretary.

To this day, some senators and staff remember her for her style, elegance, beauty, and glowing personality. Those were the days when your secretary could sit on the floor and counsel, as well as keep bills and memos in order. Frankly, we could not have functioned without them.

By 1970, the Legislature had established a process for hiring clerical staff, including the secretarial pool, that included a skills test and an interview. That's why I met Nedra Spingler, who was to have a front-row seat on my legislative activities for seven years. Much of the next narrative will be in Nedra's own words, which she reported in an interview in May 2022, when she was ninety-six. She has a memory like a steel trap, and these are her recollections of those days.

Nedra recalls meeting me for the first time at the beginning of the 1970 legislative session. On her first day on the job, she went to the Senate chambers on the third floor of the Capitol building, and saw what she said was this "young, nice-looking man holding forth with some Senate cronies." She said as she approached, I said, "You must be Nedra," and introduced her to my colleagues, adding that I got all the best-looking secretaries.

In her mind, Nedra said, "Score one for Reilly," and she decided she'd come back the next day. She shared her assessment of me, the man who was to be her boss. "He was good-looking, young, single—a spiffy dresser with suits, ties, monograms, shirts with cuff links, polished shoes." She said she knew right away, "He was going to need a housemother as well as a secretary who could handle a lot of work."

During that first year, Nedra remembers spending a lot of time "running up and down the State House stairs from the fifth-floor secretarial pool to the third-floor Senate Chambers, taking dictation, handling the mail and distracting his would-be girlfriends, and trying to find him."

According to Nedra, the would-be girlfriends had plenty of reasons. "He was young, he was nice-looking, he was a senator, he had money—or his folks had money—why wouldn't you run after him?"

Nedra said there were times when she asked herself, a forty-four-year-old secretary, why she was interfering in her thirty-three-year-old boss's love life. Still, she figured it was her job "to protect him from those he didn't want to see."

She did it as tactfully as possible: "I would just say he's not in the office, but I'll ask him to call. If he didn't call, that wasn't my problem. I was always nice to them," though she said some were more aggressive than others. "It was an eye-opener to me."

"He really had a good relationship with the Leavenworth area he represented," Nedra said. "Every day he would take *The Leavenworth Times* [the community's daily newspaper] and went through it to see if there was an article about any of his constituents, if they had done something that made news." If there were any, "I'd cut it out, and he'd write a little note himself to go with it—something like, 'I was happy to read about you in the newspaper; I am proud of you,' and he wished them the best. He always signed these letters 'With warmest personal regards, Ed Reilly.'"

And all these years later, Nedra kept one of those notes, dated on a Sunday in April 1975. Here's what she shared: "Dear Nedra, as usual the session and O'Reilly would not have been a success without your guidance and counsel and help during these trying 90 days. Although I don't say it often enough, I'm grateful. I consider myself fortunate in that I have the best secretary and public relations gal in the State House. Hope we can both endure and recover for the return on the 22nd. My best to Dick [Nedra's husband]. Fondly, Ed."

Nedra also commented on the letters I answered: "He answered every letter. Some were so shocked they'd write back and thank him." She said it was no wonder the State House postmaster told her Reilly got more mail than any other legislator.

The area's prisons were a priority, Nedra said. "If anything happened with the prisons in his area, anything they wanted to do, he was always right there for them."

The communication sometimes involved inmates. She remembered a bill passed allowing male and female inmates to intermingle. A year or two after it became law, she recalled a telephone call: "I could hear children crying in the background, and she sounded like she was at her wit's end. I said I'd be glad to have him call you in the morning." But the caller went on to say, "'My husband is in jail in Lansing and he's up for parole. But he doesn't want to leave it.'" Crying, she added, "'He's found somebody else. He's got mixed up with one of those female inmates.'" Nedra said she didn't know how the senator responded.

After what she called "this first year of initiation," I was appointed chairman of the prestigious Federal and State Affairs Committee. Nedra said, "I can't remember how he got to be chairman so soon, but he did."

Nedra took minutes for a number of interim committees that met in the summertime, so she knew how other chairmen conducted their panels. "I learned that he was one of the best. He knew what he wanted to do with a bill, and he had a way of getting measures through the committee. He aggravated some of them, but that's what he was supposed to do."

After I became chairman of the State and Federal Affairs Committee, Nedra remembers several things changing. I got an office, though she remembers that I still spent most of my time at my Senate desk. Nedra became secretary of the committee, and she said that meant she set up meetings, scheduled lobbyists and others for testimony on bills, and took minutes for all the meetings.

The death penalty was one of the major issues, but she said, "We got all the sin bills, like alcohol and gambling."

While many of the legislative secretaries left work at noon on Fridays, Nedra said she "carried on and came back most Saturday mornings to get caught up." She attributed her workload to the attention I paid to constituents.

"He answered every letter, postcard and phone call," Nedra recalled. "If a legislative bill might affect a person or group in his district, he sent them a copy, asking their opinion of it. Within his district were four prisons, and he was always on top of acts affecting their institutions and their employees and inmates." Nedra figured this was helpful in my subsequent appointment to the United States Parole Commission.

She was a great help to me. Some senators had the benefit of their wives telling them what to do, or else.

I headed the Committee on Federal and State Affairs for twenty years. If the lawyers didn't want to deal with an issue, it was likely that piece of legislation would end up at this committee. We dealt with everything you could possibly imagine—the Equal Rights amendment for women, capital punishment, abortion, all the way to medical professional recognition of midwives and chiropractors. I became one of the greatest friends of the chiropractors because I carried the bill that got them admitted for recognition by the Kansas Board of Healing Arts.

Another woman who worked with me as a secretary in the Senate was Deanna Willard. In May 2023, Deanna shared her observations.

"It was quite hectic, rushing to committee meetings, typing up minutes, organizing speakers' testimony," she wrote. She said I was "so involved in many issues; often you would ask me to 'make 10 copies of this and put them in a file.' I finally realized that it was more efficient to wait until you needed it again to make the copies. To my memory, I don't remember your needing that paper again; there was always another pressing issue to deal with. Also, you had a car phone, and on those days when you did get away at a decent time for the weekend, you would call back to the office with more instructions for Nancy and me!"

Deanna remembered that I was "always kind to everyone, no matter their position on an issue, but I'm sure no one ever moved you away from your belief on a matter! It was very interesting listening to positions on bills regarding abortion, guns, liquor, and other controversial topics. The committee room was usually full, and I felt very much a part of everything."

I was successful in most of the committee actions in passing those legislative matters. In an interview in September 2022, a colleague and friend, Democratic Senator Paul Feliciano from Wichita looked at it this way: "Ed Reilly was tenacious when it came to issues." But he also added that "when Ed Reilly didn't like a bill, he figured out ways to kill it." He had his own story of a bill that I wasn't enamored with that he was able to get passed through the committee, as he was also on the Federal and State Affairs Committee.

It passed out of committee, but Feliciano didn't think it got to general orders soon enough, which meant it could be discussed and voted on by the entire Senate. He went through the whole tedious procedure of having the president of the Senate ask me the status of the bill. He swears I told him I didn't like the bill, and I liked it less when he raised the question, and he insists I took the bill from a drawer in my office and waved it at him. But the next day I sent it to general orders.

I learned early the battles to get something passed aren't always fought on the battlefield, but rather in the halls of the Legislature, city and county government chambers, and even in the conference rooms of trustees and directors. Of course, the real battlefield was established when our Founding Fathers, through compromise, structured a government that has survived based on Western moral tradition and the sincere efforts to seek compromise with civility and respect that would be in the majority's best interest.

I think political productivity was robust in those times because most politicians were forthright about dealing with issues and people. Elected officials staked their reputation on the long-term record of making happen that which they told the electorate they would make happen. Your word was your bond. Unfortunately, today, a politician's words have much less credibility because they have much less connection to their deeds.

The same goes for journalism and the media at large. When I went to journalists like John Marshall, Roger Myers, or Lew Ferguson, I was comfortable speaking to them about issues in confidence because I knew the information would actually stay confidential, if I requested. These journalists, and others back then, were also up-front and fair about how they reported the news, so people could assess what was happening and make their own decisions.

In the media today, much credibility has been lost because so much is partisan. If people can't rely on getting unbiased and accurate news, it can harm our society. And certainly for me, since I still use several TV stations as my go-to, comparing and analyzing events is much more challenging. I can't imagine how I'd feel if I included the dozens of online and, God forbid, social media sources.

The class of '24, which consisted of both Democrats and Republicans, was elected in 1964, so we were quite close. In those days, we respected each other's opinions and performed with the courtesy and professionalism expected of a legislator. My close colleagues included two Kansas City gentlemen who were Senate leaders. Senator Norman Gaar was majority leader, and Senator Jack Steineger was minority leader. That friendship led to the opportunity to sail the Caribbean on Jack Steineger's forty-two-foot Morgan sailboat. The memories of these trips are forever in my mind, as we visited almost every island and made friends on most of them. Jack, a Naval School graduate, was an accomplished cruiser and captain, but we often found it wise to take along his cousin who lived on St. John Island and knew the waters.

We became like brothers in the bonds, and we were instrumental in convincing our colleagues to pass bills that enhanced the further development of our state. To my knowledge, there was no hidden agenda. It was all about what was best for Kansas and what was the fiscal note. Wouldn't that be a great pursuit for legislative bodies today?

3

The Issues

Each state has specific issues that its elected officials need to resolve. But all states share a common and perpetual problem: Do we have the necessary funds and resources to do what we say we're going to do? Kansas was no different, so this constant pressure on state finances meant my committee looked at bills and dealt with decisions that some Kansan found controversial.

Education needs to be funded, and the government has to keep running, whether you're talking about local, state or federal. Politicians can have good ideas about where the money should go, but few are as committed to figuring out where the money will come from. I think Governor Bob Docking understood that. Both he and his father were bankers. They were conservative, prudent, and focused on balancing the budget. As we know, "balanced budget" is not a popular topic with many politicians. Some never want to acknowledge the issue. In Washington, DC, for example, as I am writing this, talk of "only" a $1.8 trillion deficit is welcomed as good news. So during my tenure in Kansas, I introduced a bill that provided fiscal notes for the Legislature, allowing us a much easier way to estimate the cost of all these proposed programs.

My Democratic colleague, Paul Feliciano of Wichita, said before that happened, "It was hard to ascertain whether someone was blowing smoke." He was kind enough to call me a "visionary," because he thought it was prudent that legislators ask the basic questions, "What will be the cost, short-term and long-term?"

But the revenue side meant we had to get into places that some didn't want to go, like a state lottery, gambling, and horse and dog racing. We even revisited longstanding alcohol laws, and that was definitely not easy. Kansas was the first state to pass a constitutional amendment in 1880 banning the production and sale of alcohol. It's also the state with the longest period of Prohibition, from 1881 to 1948. Even after that, no one could sell liquor by the drink in their restaurants or bars; only package sales were allowed. So the "private club" system emerged in 1965 to get around these restrictions. It didn't take long for Kansas's private club issue to become a mess. Because they were private clubs, they could be opaque to those who wanted to know what was going on inside. I mean literally opaque, with painted or drape-covered windows so not even law enforcement could see the often-illicit activity.

I sometimes tell the story of taking Governor Bob Docking into downtown Kansas City, Kansas, to what was then called The Copper Kettle, across from the Townhouse Hotel. We wanted to show him firsthand what was going on in the clubs, and to impress upon him that we needed to do something about the liquor laws. Not surprisingly, a crew consisting of legislators, the governor, and his security detail was not a welcome sight. I had to threaten the doorman with a visit from the Alcoholic Beverage Control that would shut them down to get him to let us inside the club. Once inside, I think we'd made our point to the governor.

We didn't get the liquor amendment to a successful referendum vote until November 1986, at the end of Governor John Carlin's last term. But we began the effort almost a decade before. During that same session, we also voted in the State Lottery and pari-mutuel. Each county could vote to have these activities in their area. Thirty-six counties voted to have them; they were defeated in sixty-nine others. Over time, more would do so, as they realized the need to respond to what were primarily economic stressors—intrastate competition for residents (people were leaving many

Kansas areas); competition for tourists, since many of them would opt for a state where they could drink without belonging to a private club or being invited to one; business sector development (while we were still debating, Missouri was going ahead with their riverboat gambling and casinos); and revenue requirements for all the projects Kansans wanted done.

In some ways, if it weren't for the work of Senator Jack Steineger, Senator Norman Gaar, myself, and some of the other Wyandotte County legislators, there would have been no development of the Legends—a large shopping area—and Kansas City, Kansas, would not be what it is today.

The necessity to make decisions while in public service teaches you—perhaps faster than in most callings or careers—that life isn't about good or bad, but about trade-offs. I imagine the most disappointed person after the November 1986 referendum was the Reverend Richard Taylor, a Methodist minister who had been leading the anti-liquor battle in Kansas for almost two decades. Not a great fan of gambling either, he held great sway over many Kansans.

Senator Feliciano recalled that every time the liquor-by-the-drink issue came up, Reverend Taylor would stop it. "A thousand people would flood the phones of senators if it came up," he said in a September 2022 interview. He said Gaar called, wanting him to count the number of Democrats it would take to pass the bill. As minority whip, he had the numbers, and he urged Gaar to get me to talk to Republican Senator Ben Vidricksen of Salina to secure his vote. Gaar urged Feliciano to be ready at 9:30 that night. Gaar asked Feliciano if he saw Reverend Taylor anywhere in the Senate chambers. Feliciano said he'd been looking for him, too, but he understood he was in Nebraska. Gaar told him Taylor was giving a speech in Nebraska, so it was time to run the bill. Feliciano remembered that Senate President Ross Doyen "was livid. He was doing everything but calling the Highway Patrol to bring Taylor back." Vidricksen agreed to vote for the measure if Feliciano voted for a measure he wanted passed, which the latter agreed to, and the measure passed with a twenty-two-vote margin.

I think the finance issue also made a difference. Once we explained what was going on in the private clubs, I think they understood that it couldn't continue. People were getting hurt.

Like legislators, Reverend Taylor was also looking at data to support his stance. Although religious views of sin were likely the main impetus behind his efforts, he was also concerned about the rise in alcoholism and domestic violence. In addition, he worried about traffic-accident-related deaths. All were legitimate concerns. There's no question that the activities resulting from some of the laws we passed could and did lead to misfortune in some people's lives. Public servants should never lose sight of that.

On the other hand, I've spoken to many people who told me they want to be able to do things they enjoy. Those who want to go into public service, maybe politics, will have to grapple with plenty of thorny problems. Who should decide what I can and cannot do with my earnings on my own time? When does the state or local government have a right to regulate my choices? How do we balance the rights of an individual with those of a community? Or desires for future growth while maintaining the stability of a group, a state, a nation or so on?

While we were talking horse and dog races, we also wanted Kansas to have the first riverboat for gambling. We even had a riverboat on the Kansas River that a gentleman from Kansas City, Kansas, was willing to develop as a casino going up and down the river. We couldn't get that included, though, because the horse and dog people were fighting with each other. Otherwise, we'd have gotten a jump on Missouri.

Simple talk of "good" versus "bad" disappears rapidly for those who approach these issues with the complexity and the maturity they deserve. You have to make tough decisions, and you have to stand behind them, as you will be held accountable for them. Especially at the state level, I believe legislators can be successful if they're intimately involved with local officials, because this will help them really understand the questions they're asked to resolve. I'm not sure enough of that happens today.

* * * * *

Prison labor was another controversial issue. During the 1930s, using inmates in private companies was considered exploitative. But by the late 1970s, Congress was more amenable to the idea, mostly as a response to surging prison populations and finding better ways for rehabilitation efforts. Criminal justice in Kansas, when I entered the public square, was based on a punitive model. This changed with the appearance of Dr. Karl Menninger of the famous Menninger Foundation, associated for a long time with the Topeka State Hospital. Dr. Menninger, through his consulting work for the US Bureau of Prisons and the Topeka Police Department, was able to convince the Legislature to pursue a new course of action. He envisioned providing tools, such as mental health resources and alcohol counseling, to offer new opportunities in life through rehabilitation.

But incentives in the private sector also found their way into prison rehabilitation applications. A mindset for economic development created a space for entrepreneurs to bring solutions and improvements to Kansas. One entrepreneur was Fred Braun, who bought three failing manufacturing companies and brought them to Leavenworth. He wanted them to be staffed with inmates from the Kansas State Penitentiary and from the women's prison, which at the time was in Lansing. Braun believed that for someone incarcerated, employment, especially outside the prison setting, was an important element of rehabilitation. These activities not only helped the inmates who made minimum wage, they also created revenue for the state and for victim restitution.

To this day, we are training prisoners in Leavenworth, Kansas to make snowplows, machinery parts, heating elements, and other equipment. This has become a national model, and, through the Workman Fund, Braun supported the expansion of this model to other private companies around the country to employ, educate, and rehabilitate inmates. This opportunity for prisoners to work outside prison walls would not have existed if we hadn't thought through the tradeoffs for each group and passed the necessary legislation for the Department of Corrections to engage.

But when you serve in the Kansas Legislature, and you're from Leavenworth, you will inevitably have to deal with that other side of the prison system. Among my files from that time is a list of the inmates murdered while they were doing their time at Kansas State Penitentiary. There were twenty-three from the period of 1976 to August 1992, when I left to come to Washington: in-cell burnings, stabbings, beatings with baseball bats, people thrown off cellblock tiers. They were in for anything from kidnapping, to burglary and robbery, to murder. But as an inmate, when you go to prison, you like to think you're going to serve your time and hopefully even change your behavior or rehabilitate yourself. Unfortunately, that's not always the case.

My Senate colleague Paul Feliciano, who served on the Federal and State Affairs Committee, recalls a time when riots were occurring at the state prison, and I decided some of us needed to have a firsthand look at what was going on. I asked him what he had planned for the afternoon, and he mentioned a couple of assignments. I said, "No, you don't. Come on. We're leaving," and five or six of us, including Senators Gaar, Steineger, and Wes Sowers, took off in my car.

"When we got to the prison, they didn't want to let us in because they were having problems," Feliciano said. "Ed talked to the Highway Patrol, and said, 'We want an escort. We want some of your officers with us. We're going in, and we want to see what the problems are.'"

We got inside and wanted to go to the lowest level, where the worst prisoners were housed. The Highway Patrol thought we'd be putting ourselves in harm's way and they didn't want to be responsible for us. So I said, "OK, we'll compromise. Get some officers, and we'll be on one end of the cell." Feliciano and I remember that we finally met with some inmates in one of the barbershops. The inmates outlined some issues, including what they said was lousy food and food that was sabotaged, like prisoners spitting in it. We told them we'd meet with the warden and see if we could effectuate any changes.

"Things calmed down quite a bit after that," Feliciano remembers. "I think the inmates were shocked that state senators would meet with them and take time out of our busy schedule to talk to them, and that we'd talk to them without the Highway Patrol being right by our side. This just exemplifies the kind of leader Reilly was."

Another issue legislators learned about was the mutilations Lansing inmates committed on themselves, especially of the Achilles tendon. An orthopedic surgeon in Leavenworth performed numerous surgeries sewing up self-inflicted cuts. Eventually, prison officials determined the self-mutilations were just an excuse to get out of prison and into a community hospital, even if the inmates were cuffed and constantly guarded by a Lansing officer. Warden Ray Gaffney decided to put a stop to it, and every time an officer brought an inmate headed for the hospital, he sent them back to the Lansing infirmary. In fact, there are stories that he stood by the gate with a shotgun over his shoulder if an inmate was on his way to the hospital for such treatment. Today that strong stand would result in a slew of litigation. And self-mutilations still occur in correctional institutions, no doubt for the same reasons.

One story that circulated about the state prison was about the "tunnel of love." Everyone was interested in how you could have a tunnel like that to the women's prison, which was staffed by female custodial officers. But according to the story, the men working at the boiler plant were able to crawl through the steam tunnel under the highway that separated the plant from the prison. The heating plant provided heat not only to the men's prison, but also to the women's prison, and a tunnel with the duct work ran between the two institutions. It must have been the scene for some conjugal activity, because one or two of the women prisoners allegedly got pregnant.

According to a May 9, 1957, article in *The Wichita Eagle,* state prison officials discounted parts of that story. They did acknowledge that Thomas Hernando Cotton and his prison sweetheart, Martha Stachura, used the tunnel in some way during their underground romance and ultimate escape on December 29, 1956, but they point out the steam tunnel was so unbearably hot most people would want out within a few minutes. Daisy Sharpe, the superintendent of the women's industrial farm, said she could provide proof that the twenty-seven-year-old Mrs. Stachura was not pregnant when she escaped. The woman, who was married to another prisoner, twenty-year-old Edgar Stachura, told reporters when the couple was captured in California that she was pregnant because of their steamy trysts.

The two escapees also told reporters wild parties were common in the Lansing prisons. Cotton, also known as Hernando, "told a tale of vice and orgies in the prison, including marijuana and drinking parties, as well as romancing by men and women prisoners," the *Eagle* reported.

Tracy Hand, who had just taken over as warden of the men's prison, said marijuana was always a problem in the summer because hemp, the natural form of marijuana, grows wild in Kansas. It is plentiful on the prison's several thousands of acres of hills and fields, many of which were worked by the prisoners. Officers searched the workers before they came inside, but often found it in their pant cuffs. The prison bought bulk tobacco, and most of the male prisoners rolled their own cigarettes and could easily roll the hemp in with the tobacco.

By the time the *Eagle* reporter was allowed inside the tunnel, one opening had been covered by a heavy concrete slab. The other end was blocked by a heavy steel grill and a padlock, and there was a steel door in the tunnel, thus closing what has been dubbed the "Tunnel of Love."

During my Kansas public service, I've had the opportunity to become a lot more educated about what really goes on in an institution, besides all the sex and drugs and assaults. I remember US Senator Bob Dole saying, "If anybody should be chairman of the Federal Parole Commission, it should be Ed Reilly." And that was simply because I happened to be born in Leavenworth.

Prison reform is an issue that you can look at and say, "The more things change, the more they stay the same." In tracking criminal justice issues, I've observed a thirty-year cycle, and issues that play out nationally obviously impact the states. Money is always tied to the issue. Nationally today we're taking the positions that we want to let more people out, and we don't want to lock as many people up. The talk turns to rehabilitating people, and all this sounds wonderful when you're trying to sell something, but it all goes back to money and having the finances to do what you're talking about.

Kansas is like everywhere else—you can throw a concept out for debate, but you need to know how you're going to fund it. I've learned from different sources that some programs we pushed through for prison reform have been cut back because of funding cuts. But they're cutting the nose off their face out of spite because it's not keeping people out of institutions.

* * * * *

While I was a Kansas senator, years before my service as chairman of the United States Parole Commission, I was selected to serve as a commissioner on the Accreditation for Law Enforcement Agencies Commission. Formed in 1979, the commission developed a set of law enforcement standards based on best practices and administered a voluntary accreditation process. As I reflect on that experience today, I can see it helped prepare me for the work on the US Parole Commission.

Through the accreditation process, law enforcement agencies at state, county, and local levels could demonstrate they met professional criteria. The twenty-one-member commission reflected a broad representation of practitioners in law enforcement from departments of various sizes. Also included were representatives from the public and private sectors to include justices, senators, county administrators, mayors and council members, and professors of criminal justice.

Leavenworth County Sheriff Terry Campbell nominated me to serve on the panel. Serving with me were representatives of numerous groups, including the International Association of Chiefs of Police; the National Organization of Black Law Enforcement Executives; the National Sheriffs Association; and the Police Executive Research Forum. The groups represented 80 percent of the law enforcement community of the United States.

The panel developed one thousand standards that were researched and tested to cover the diversity of law enforcement responsibilities.

These policies and practices have guided many agencies since 1979 with what are believed to be best practices.

Today, if we see municipalities having major problems, we can ask if that city or area's law enforcement agencies are accredited. It is a process of seeking improvement and change in the conduct while creating a structure by which they can upgrade their services as professionally as possible to help the public. I have been disappointed to witness what is happening in many major metropolitan communities today, in many cases because they aren't following established standards and best practices.

As I reflect on the opportunities I had because of my positions in public service, I feel I have earned the equivalent of several degrees through all the exposure.

* * * * *

Another topic that was a constant in the Kansas Legislature was gun legislation. Then, as well as now, I'm a strong proponent of the Second Amendment, the right to carry and bear arms. Even before I was in the Legislature, I was a reserve deputy sheriff in Leavenworth County. I've had a permit and carried a weapon most of my life. Besides other law enforcement training, I attended training at the state's law enforcement academy near Hutchinson. The Kansas Peace Officer Association sponsored the school. When I was with the United States Parole Commission, I was a deputy US marshal. Again, I got a permit and attended the US Marshal school. I carried a weapon primarily for personal protection there because of the job. So I'm definitely a strong proponent of the Second Amendment.

When I was in the Legislature, people on farms were driving around with rifles mounted in the back windows of their pickup trucks. The issue was up for debate, but you didn't have open carry, which is now legal in Kansas. The state has come a long way in legalizing the right to bear arms.

Living in Kansas gave me a great opportunity to develop my strong values in commitment to the Constitution, the principles of the Founding Fathers, and the desire to preserve the American way of life. Coming from a business and a political family, I was taught by example the importance of truth, integrity, compassion, commitment, and concern for the welfare of others. The passing of the torch allowed me to serve in the administrations of five governors and five presidents, and ultimately, I'll face the Being to whom I will be most accountable to at the end of my tenure on earth.

My family has always subscribed to the philosophy of service to others. There's a saying that should apply to all of us: "The service we perform on earth is the rent we pay for the space we each occupy." As we look at where we are in 2024, we should be mindful of how blessed we are and why we need to repeat these words often, as we owe a great deal to our nation. Service in the Kansas Legislature was a marvelous experience, as I worked with legislators from all parts of our Sunflower State who were dedicated and committed to doing what was right for their fellow Kansans. And all that happened in those Kansas chambers proved to be a great education for what was to come in Washington, DC.

4

Capital Punishment

Capital punishment was one of the most controversial issues that repeatedly came up in the Federal and State Affairs Committee when I was chairman. I felt passionate about this issue; I couldn't have carried the bill otherwise. It became very real to me after I was one of two legislators the governor picked to witness the next-to-last executions in Kansas, those of Richard Hickock and Perry Smith in 1965. This became one of the most famous cases in Kansas when Truman Capote wrote about the murders of the Clutter family in Holcomb in his 1966 nonfiction novel, *In Cold Blood*, which was also made into a film.

The death penalty has been abolished and reinstated three times in Kansas. Governor Edward Hoch first abolished it on January 30, 1907; it was reinstated in 1935, but no executions occurred until 1944. This death penalty statute was in effect until the 1972 US Supreme Court ruling that struck it down. After its constitutionality was reinstated in 1976, the Kansas Legislature voted numerous times to reinstate it, but Governor John Carlin vetoed it in 1979, 1980, 1981, and 1985. The current death penalty statute was enacted when Governor Joan Finney allowed it to become law without her signature in 1994—after I was already in Washington, DC.

I know a great number of my papers now filed at the Spencer Research Library at the University of Kansas include testimony and letters I received on this topic—arguments for and against the reinstatement of capital punishment.

As I reflect on my Catholic education and upbringing, I am well aware of the dangers of sentencing someone to death; the criminal justice system has made mistakes, which we now find more frequently with the advent of technology, especially DNA. I also know many leaders of my faith believe the death penalty is not the right answer. I have found, though, that at least some priests and a number of Catholic laymen understand my arguments.

My religious formation and public service, especially in the Legislature, tell me we have a duty to protect the lives of our citizens, including those we incarcerate. I learned early on about the terrible things that can happen to the inmate who's learned a lesson and just wants to return to society and live a better life. At the same time, we can't forget that the men and women who serve us in the corrections institutions are entitled to life, liberty and the continued pursuit of happiness. All too often our correctional staff have been victims of atrocities. They've been stabbed, burned, had feces flung at them, been raped and assaulted, and been bitten by inmates with HIV who want to contaminate them.

I believe the death penalty can be a deterrent, and I know of one example that occurred when I was in the Legislature. Kansas had the death penalty at that time and the adjoining state, Missouri, did not. Two men picked up a woman on the Missouri side of the river that separates the states. They violently raped and brutalized her before driving her across the river and releasing her in Kansas. One of the predators convinced his accomplice not to kill the woman and throw her over the bridge because he realized Kansas had the death penalty.

* * * * *

The heinous murders of the Clutter family occurred when Kansas had the death penalty. The two murderers, Richard Hickock and Perry Smith, fled the scene with only a Zenith table radio, a pair of binoculars, and forty dollars—not the huge sum they'd been told Clutter kept at his home. Both had been incarcerated at Kansas State Penitentiary, and Hickock's cellmate, Floyd Wells, had been a farmhand for Clutter.

He told them Clutter was wealthy and kept a great deal of money in a safe at his home.

Wells encouraged the two to rob this rich farmer when they got out of prison. That was their plan when they drove four hundred miles across the state on the night of November 14, 1959. They reached the Clutter farmstead early the next morning and entered the unlocked door of the home, where Herb Clutter and his wife Bonnie were sleeping. Their sixteen-year-old daughter, Nancy, and fifteen-year-old son, Kenyon, were also asleep in upstairs bedrooms.

They offered the thief's typical promise: "We just want the money you have hidden here; give it to us, and we won't harm you." However, not many smart Kansas farmers keep their money at home or buried in the haystack. Herb Clutter was a successful and well-liked resident of Finney County, and all his money was in the bank. Hickock and Smith tied up the family members, and it became obvious they had more in mind than robbery.

When they couldn't find the safe Wells had promised was there, they realized their haul would be only the radio, the binoculars, and the forty dollars. Things turned ugly. They slit Herb Clutter's throat and left him to die, then shot his son and his wife point-blank with a shotgun and attempted to rape his daughter. However, they finally put her out of her misery and shot her in the head too. It was one of Kansas's most brutal crimes, and the Kansas Bureau of Investigation was called in to assist local officials. Had it not been for the inmate at the state prison who'd heard the discussion between Hickock and Smith, they might well have escaped the hangman. Because of that information, they were arrested in Las Vegas six weeks later, on December 30. Finney County authorities quickly arraigned them, and they were speedily convicted. They were executed five years later at the state prison, where they'd previously spent time.

One morning in Kansas, more than forty-seven years ago now, I woke to a message from Governor Bill Avery calling me to his office for a meeting. When I arrived, I found a colleague from the Senate, Jack Barr. He was a Kansas movie star if we ever had one—right out of the West and a successful rancher from Leoti, Kansas. This meeting was in 1965, when Richard Hickock and Perry Smith were scheduled to be executed. During that time, debates were still going on about whether the Kansas death penalty should be repealed.

Our meeting with the governor was rather brief; he was in the throes of trying to decide whether capital punishment should continue in the state. He requested both of us attend Hickock and Smith's executions as his representative. Governor Avery was interested in our observations in view of the ongoing death penalty debate. Although taken aback by the governor's request, we accepted. The Barrs and Clutters were neighbors, and I was the senator from the Third District, where the prison is located.

The evening of April 16, 1965, was terribly rainy when Senator Barr and I traveled the hour or so to Lansing from Topeka, the state capital. We met author Truman Capote for the first time that night. At that time, he was not famous or well known outside his own environment. Capote had befriended both Hickock and Smith during regular visits with them as he crafted his story about the men and their crime for *In Cold Blood*. I thought Capote was a strange gentleman, and he wore extremely thick tinted glasses. I'm not sure whether he wore a sports jacket or a suit, but I definitely remember the glasses. He wasn't very communicative—rather, he was quiet and subdued. I could appreciate that, because we were all on our best behavior.

Barr, Capote, and I all rode in the same car from the warden's office to the warehouse just outside the prison, where the gallows were located. Over the years, I've often been asked about my impressions of Capote; I've determined he was what you might expect of a man who used two poor souls to gain fame and fortune through his book and movie detailing the case. Some believe the experience had such an impact on him he found himself unable to write anything of substance afterwards. I think something like that could weigh on you, as you realize your success came by taking advantage of broken souls with no conscience who couldn't make it as valuable members of society. That type of exploitation doesn't stop. I fully expect someone to use the 2022 University of Idaho murder case to write a book about the mass killing of four bright college students whose whole lives stretched before them with the potential of contributing to society.

But thinking back to the execution at Lansing—I was there to witness something that I never thought that I'd be called upon to see, which itself was a shock. That warehouse was a frightening scene, with the gallows located in a corner. I had imagined it would be a more professional room, rather than a warehouse where lumber and other prison supplies were stored. And it was very emotional going inside with Capote.

When we got there, Warden Sherman Crouse was already there, as were the Reverend James Post, the prison chaplain, and the appropriate number of correctional staff. Officer Jerry Collins was pretty much the head guy who knew what to do.

The clock was almost at midnight when Hickock, the first to be hanged, was brought to the building, driven in with three corrections officers accompanying him. Warden Crouse, a close personal friend of mine, read the death order and made the usual request asking whether Hickock would like to speak. One thing that consoled me was that neither man denied they'd committed the horrible act for which they were now paying their lives. Hickock thanked the warden and Capote as well as Reverend Post. His last words were, "I don't have any hard feelings; you're sending me to a better place." He also said he was sorry for what they had done, and he forgave us for what we were about to do. I have never forgotten that message. Smith was hanged a little later, and he used his last words to say that capital punishment was legally and morally wrong. He also forgave us for what we were doing.

Both inmates are buried at Mount Muncie Cemetery in Lansing, as their families did not claim the bodies. Hickock donated his eyes, which resulted in sight for a young girl waiting at the University of Kansas Medical Center. Former correctional officer Collins remembered the Kansas Highway Patrol rushing the eyes to the KU Medical Center after two doctors removed them at the Davis Funeral Chapel. So at least one of the inmates gave something back to society for the violence they inflicted on a well-known Kansas farm family. Kansas, as a Midwestern state, is not very tolerant of those who commit violent acts.

I met with former correctional officer Jerry Collins on July 26, 2012, while I was working on this book and recalling Truman Capote. Also at that meeting were former Kansas Bureau of Investigation Director Larry Welch and Agent Larry Thomas, the assistant director. Collins had worked at Kansas State Penitentiary for many years, and he had a wealth of information about Truman Capote and the Hickock and Smith executions. He had retained a lot of notes, articles and photos that helped tell the story that made Capote famous. This meeting was a chance for me to compare what I thought I experienced and saw versus what I'd forgotten in the years since that momentous night.

Collins had many contacts with both Hickock and Smith and also escorted each man on the night of their execution. He talked about the last meal requests both men made and the effort the warden made to supply the meals they wanted, making arrangements with the famous Savoy Grill in Kansas City, Missouri. The Savoy is known as the place where former President Harry Truman often dined, and a booth is even dedicated to him as it was his usual seat. The Savoy specializes in seafood, and they both requested a complete lobster meal with some beef thrown in. The prison sent a vehicle to Kansas City, thirty miles away, to supply the last meal. In my opinion, it was a waste of good lobster.

Collins confirmed what I'd observed: Capote got sick after the first man, Hickock, was hanged, and he went behind a lumber pile in the warehouse to throw up. Collins believed Capote then asked Warden Sherman Crouse to be excused so he could leave. He didn't remember if the warden approved, but my memory is that the warden said, "You may not leave, as you are an official witness."

To my knowledge, he was not permitted to leave the warehouse, but he did turn around so as not to face the gallows when inmate Smith was brought in for execution. According to Collins, Smith hung for more than eighteen minutes because his neck did not break, and he was strangled.

My observation was that both men hung for anywhere from eighteen to twenty minutes, and I didn't recognize any struggling other than the normal reflexes in death. Both inmates were hooked up to a heart monitor, which the attending physician listened to; he declared them dead when the heart ceased to beat.

Davis Moulden, the local undertaker, drove the hearse into the building and removed both bodies. After the first execution, the rope was cut, and the noose was left on the inmate's neck. When Davis put him on the cot to roll him out, the noose was still there. They put up another rope to carry out the second execution. Davis and I both remembered a miserable night of rain and an eerie quiet that came over the institution.

It was a real awakening as to the penalty for the most heinous crimes. For me, going to the federal prison as a young man and later witnessing the executions amounted to a "Scared Straight" treatment; I would never think of violating the law and going to a penitentiary. When it comes to prison, you hope the punishments you mete out are deterrents—otherwise, you're wasting your ink and paper. But I really believe capital punishment should be the penalty for the most violent crimes, for those with no respect for human life.

At the time, I did not think watching two men be hanged should have been part of my charge as a senator, but as I reflect back, Barr and I had the obligation as legislators to educate ourselves on the process and to report our counsel to the governor as he requested. I'm often asked if I would do this again, and I promptly respond that there's no need to do so. Kansas did reinstate the death penalty after the Supreme Court struck it down in the Furman v. Georgia case, and it remains the law of the state today, not by hanging, but by lethal injection.

When I interviewed Officer Collins, I had many questions. One related to a call I received from New York's famous author, George Plimpton, regarding an article he was writing for the October 30, 1997, edition of *The New Yorker* concerning Truman Capote. He had been told by a former Kansas Bureau of Investigation agent that the two inmates were having a physical love affair with Capote. Plimpton wanted to confirm what I knew.

In *The New Yorker* article, Harold Nye, former assistant director of the Kansas Bureau of Investigation, said he'd gotten his information from an FBI agent who had since died.

In a November 23, 1997, article in *The Leavenworth Times*, Charles McAtee, director of penal institutions for Kansas from 1964–1969, insisted otherwise. "It's bovine fecal matter," he said. "It never happened; it could not have happened."

Collins agreed. He had worked in what was then called Segregation and Isolation or Death Row, which was on the second row of the cell block. "The way S & I was laid out, it would have been impossible."

He described Death Row as having a piece of plywood going down the center to separate the two sides. He said an officer's desk was at the end, and an officer was sitting there all the time. There was also an institution rule: "You couldn't open a death row cell unless four officers were present," Collins added.

I declined an invitation to appear on *Larry King Live*, along with McAtee and Jack Barr, where Plimpton would also be a guest. But I agree with McAtee. I knew enough people at the prison that I'm sure I would have heard of it if it had occurred.

Witnessing executions like this was a reminder to me that my own education afforded me direction on how you should live and treat others, especially employing the Ten Commandments and other Biblical lessons. But I also recognized there are fractured human beings who go astray and have little conscience about their actions. The person without a conscience doesn't distinguish between right and wrong.

*****

There are more than enough examples of this, but let's consider the executions that occurred just before and just after Hickock and Smith.

Upon seeing a photo of Lowell Lee Andrews, an eighteen-year-old University of Kansas student from the small town of Wolcott near Lansing, you'd be hard-pressed to think of him as a murderer. Andrews, a sophomore zoology major who played bassoon in the college band, was described in his hometown newspaper as the "nicest boy in Wolcott."

In Episode 175 of the *Fresh Hell* podcast released in 2022, the American and Austrian podcasters refer to Andrews as a "family annihilator." They note that Andrews's parents, who were reasonably well-to-do, had no reason to suspect their son was making plans to kill them. In fact, he'd been a well-behaved son and had not caused problems. Later it was learned that the murders had been planned, probably beginning sometime in the summer of 1958. Later that year, in November, Lowell Lee and his sister Jennie Marie were home for the Thanksgiving holiday. As his sister and his parents watched television, Lowell Lee went upstairs to finish a novel. Then, he came downstairs carrying a .22 caliber rifle and a German Luger.

He shot his twenty-year-old sister between the eyes with the rifle. He turned the gun on his father, shooting him twice and his mother three times. When his mother moved toward him, he shot her three more times. When his father attempted to crawl into the kitchen, he shot him repeatedly, for a total of seventeen shots.

Andrews then drove back to his apartment in Lawrence—he would later claim to police he needed to pick up his typewriter to write an essay. After watching a movie at the Granada Theater, he drove to the Massachusetts Street Bridge, where he dismantled the weapons and threw them into the Kansas River. He then drove back home and called the police to inform them of a robbery at his parents' house.

He proclaimed his innocence until the family minister, Pastor Vertio C. Dameron of the Grandview Baptist Church in Kansas City, Kansas, talked to him. Dameron was not only their minister but a close family friend, as he'd grown up on a Missouri farm adjacent to Andrews's father. At the sheriff's office, the minister initially consoled Lowell Lee about the deaths and told him since he'd known him all his life, he couldn't believe he had anything to do with the crimes. However, multiple sources indicate he next said, "Lee, you didn't do this, did you?" Andrews said he did.

In an interview reported in *The Lawrence Journal World*, Andrews said, "I'm not sorry and I'm not glad I did it. I just don't know why I did it. I didn't even feel anything as they died."

Though he pleaded not guilty by reason of insanity, he was convicted and sentenced to death for the three murders. Kansas Governor John Anderson Jr. denied his request for clemency, and he was hanged on November 30, 1962.

* * * * *

The last hangings on the KSP gallows were those of George Ronald York and James Latham, on June 22, 1965. The two met at Fort Hood, Texas, where they were privates in the United States Army. York, who grew up in Florida, was eighteen when they met in the Fort Hood Stockade; Latham was nineteen. Both went AWOL, wandering away from a stockade work detail on May 24, 1961, and walking into Louisiana.

They set out for York's Florida home and within two weeks, they'd killed seven people on a cross-country killing spree. They'd intended to kill one more man, Edward Guidroz, who stopped to pick up the two hitchhikers on his way home from a fish market. They beat him, stole his truck and left him for dead in a Baton Rouge cemetery, but he didn't die.

On their scythe-shaped route across the country, they killed three women—two in Georgia and an eighteen-year-old hotel maid in Colorado, whom they molested and murdered. Their victims also included four men, whom they robbed and shot to death. They deserted their first stolen vehicle and stole a car. They shot a man who ran a gas station, killing him and stealing some gasoline. The male victims were in Tennessee, Illinois, and Kansas. They shot sixty-two-year-old Otto Ziegler to death in Wallace, Kansas on June 9 and took his wallet.

The smiling faces of the teenage murderers were flashed on front pages everywhere after their arrest, and the Associated Press reported those who knew them described them as "nice kids."

The two were hanged on the gallows at Kansas State Penitentiary on June 22, 1965. Latham's last words were reported as, "I'm not mad at anybody." York, hanged last, said, "There is nothing to say but that I'm going to heaven."

Theirs were the last hangings in Kansas. As of June 2016, the *Lawrence Journal-World* reported ten inmates were on death row at the El Dorado Correctional Facility, awaiting lethal injection.

* * * * *

The status of the death penalty in Kansas had shifted several times in the decades before Governor Joan Finney allowed it to become law without her signature in 1994. Because of those shifts, one of the most prolific serial killers in the state, Dennis Rader, received ten life sentences without the chance of parole for ten vicious murders he committed between 1974 and 1991. He was arrested in February 2005, and he remains in solitary confinement at the El Dorado Correctional Facility.

His first victims were the Oteros, a Wichita family. On January 15, 1974, Rader killed the thirty-eight-year-old father, the thirty-three-year-old mother and their nine-year-old son and eleven-year-old daughter. The three older children found their bodies upon arriving home from school. They were the first to endure the binding, torture and killing that led to him dubbing himself the BTK killer in a letter to the media after subsequent killings. This trademark stuck.

Between the spring of 1974 and the winter of 1977, he killed three women: Kathryn Bright in April 1974, Shirley Vian Relford in March 1977, and Nancy Fox in December 1977. In early 1978, he sent a letter to a Wichita TV station, KAKE, taking credit for all the murders and suggesting the name BTK. Several women he intended to kill managed to evade him, Rader confessed later.

He was successful in killing a neighbor, fifty-three-year-old Marine Hedge, whose body was discovered on May 5, 1985, in an area between North Webb and North Greenwich roads. Later, he confessed he'd killed her on April 27 and then taken her dead body to Christ Lutheran Church, where he was president of the church council. He photographed her body in various bondage positions and wrapped her in black plastic sheets and other equipment he'd previously stored at the church in preparation for this ritual.

The two other victims were Vicki Wegerle, killed in her home in 1986, and Dolores E. Davis, found on February 1, 1991, in Park City, where Rader worked for the city as a dog catcher and compliance officer. Rader led a double life for more than three decades. To the public and his wife and two children, he was a normal father who participated in normal activities. Besides being president of his church council, he was a Cub Scout leader. Among other jobs, Rader had worked for the Coleman Company and a home security company prior to his job for Park City.

When an FBI agent knocked at her door in 2005, his daughter Kerri Rawson, who was married and living in Michigan, couldn't believe the father she knew had confessed to ten murders. In 2019, she told her story in a book, *A Serial Killer's Daughter: My Story of Faith, Love, and Overcoming*.

Throughout his journey of murderous horror that terrified Wichita residents for years, Rader taunted law enforcement and the media with numerous letters and photos detailing his horrific deeds. Much of his correspondence was directed specifically to the BTK task force, according to a book by former KBI director Larry Welch, *Beyond Cold Blood: The KBI from Ma Barker to BTK*. Welch provides many of the gruesome details that were studied by the task force, including some graphic photos from the murders. Among these were Polaroid shots of the victims in various stages of bondage, often after they were dead, as well as shots of Rader himself dressed in lingerie he'd stolen from the victims. That way, he explained, he could relive the crimes and in so doing, satisfy his perverted sexual tastes.

Welch also recounts the judicial hearing where families of the victims were invited to listen to what Rader had told the interrogators from the task force about each of the murders. He says that it was only when Rader realized their total repugnance to his acts that he lost a bit of his bravado and arrogance about what he'd done. He pleaded guilty on June 27, 2005.

On her Twitter account, Rader's daughter speculated whether suspected Idaho killer Bryan Kohberger may have had some contact with her father. Kohberger, a twenty-eight-year-old PhD student in criminology at Washington State University, has been charged with four murders in the stabbing deaths of four University of Idaho students. The three women, Madison Mogen, twenty-one; Kaylee Goncalves, twenty-one; and Xana Kernodle, twenty, were roommates in a Moscow, Idaho, house, and they and Kernodle's boyfriend, Ethan Chapin, twenty, were brutally stabbed early in the morning of November 13, 2022, in their home. Their home was about eight miles from Washington State University. Kohberger was arrested December 30, 2022. Since then, he has accepted a plea bargain to avoid the death penalty. His story is the subject of a book underway by James Patterson as well as several TV shows.

In a Twitter post on December 31, 2022, Rawson wrote that Dr. Katherine Ramsland was one of Bryan Kohberger's professors in criminology studies at DeSales University, where he'd earned a master's degree the previous spring. She said Ramsland had had a "close academic relationship and friendship with my father, Dennis Rader, BTK."

In another Tweet that day, Rawson said she had concerns, "knowing how common it is for criminology students, true crime fans, and others to correspond regularly with my father, that Kohberger could have been in content with my father at some point, but require proof of this, which currently I do not know of."

Rader also earned a degree in criminology at Wichita State University in 1979, leading to speculation he used his degree to learn more about law enforcement methodology. I also wonder if the timing of his murders had anything to do with the suspension of the death penalty during those years.

* * * * *

The death penalty was in effect during another Kansas murder spree, often called the Wichita Massacre, involving two Dodge City brothers in their early twenties, Jonathan and Reginald Carr. Former KBI agent and criminal profiler Candice DeLong narrated an episode about the killings, "Killer Psyche: The Wichita Massacre," on her podcast, *Killer Psyche*, in February 2022. DeLong provided insights into the abusive home life and subsequent alcoholism both lived through, beginning early in their childhood. She made it clear this is not an excuse for their December 2000 killing spree, but it does help explain it. They were convicted in 2002 for this weeklong spree of random robberies, rapes, five murders, and two attempted murders. In *Beyond Cold Blood*, Welch writes that most of the Carr brothers' victims were women, and they were targeted primarily because they were driving newer vehicles in east Wichita.

Their first victim was twenty-three-year-old Andrew Schreiber, an assistant baseball coach. Their crimes against him on December 8, 2000, included carjacking, abduction, and ATM robbery, but he survived. Their violence escalated three days later as they followed fifty-five-year-old Ann Walenta, a cellist and librarian, home from a rehearsal with the Wichita Symphony. The Carr brothers followed her into her driveway and demanded at gunpoint that she get out of her sport utility vehicle. When she tried to escape by putting her vehicle in reverse and trying to leave, her assailant fired three rounds with a .380 semiautomatic pistol. One round pierced her left lung, and another severed her spinal cord, paralyzing her from the waist down.

As they fled, she described her assailant to a neighbor, who called 911. She repeated her experience to emergency responders, her husband, and Wichita police. She identified Reginald Carr from a photo array police brought to the hospital as she clung to life. However, she died of these wounds three weeks later.

On the evening of December 14, 2000, Welch recounts, the brothers were cruising east Wichita to find another likely victim. They spotted a blonde woman who had left her restaurant job in a BMW automobile to go home to her apartment triplex on Birchwood Drive. Probably because of poor visibility on that dark, snowy night, the Carr brothers knocked on the wrong door. Three friends shared that three-bedroom apartment: Jason Befort, twenty-six, a science teacher and coach; Brad Heyka, twenty-seven, an employee of Koch Industries; and Aaron Sander, twenty-nine, who was preparing to enter the seminary to become a Catholic priest. Also in the apartment when the Carr brothers knocked were Heather Muller, twenty-five, a preschool teacher, and Befort's intended fiancée, a twenty-five-year-old woman identified only as Holly G.—the unlikely survivor of that horrific night.

They forced the victims to strip, tied them up, repeatedly raped the women, and forced the five to have sex with each other. The brothers drove them to ATM machines to empty their bank accounts, and finally, drove them to a soccer field in a rural area of northeast Wichita. There the five, who were mostly unclothed, were forced to kneel in the snow in a line together. The Carr brothers shot them each in the back of the head, execution-style, Welch reports.

The bullet intended for Holly G. was deflected because of a plastic barrette she'd put in her hair shortly before the attack. Even though the Carr brothers drove their Dodge truck over her, the courageous young woman ran a mile, naked and bleeding, to the nearest home, where the occupants notified police. She provided detailed descriptions of the men to police, and her testimony was crucial in the Carr brothers' 2002 trial.

Police arrested the men on December 15, 2000, in Wichita, and they were in the Sedgwick County Jail until their trial began in October 2002. The jury found Reginald Carr guilty of fifty counts and his brother guilty of forty-three counts and recommended the death penalty, which the judge imposed. Their joint trial was later cited among challenges to the Kansas Supreme Court and then to the US Supreme Court.

Their attorneys have mounted numerous challenges over the years. In 2014, the Kansas Supreme Court overturned their death sentences on two grounds, one being the trial before a single jury violated the Eighth Amendment. In essence, the ruling said the jury was exposed to prejudicial information about the other brother when each was allowed to present mitigating circumstances to spare his life. The court also ruled the trial judge's instructions to the jury were unconstitutional because they failed to note that the brothers weren't required to prove mitigating evidence beyond a reasonable doubt.

But two years later, in 2016, the US Supreme Court reversed those rulings and returned the cases to the Kansas high court for resolution.

In May 2021 the brothers went before the Kansas Supreme Court once again. In January 2022 the court upheld their challenge that the death penalty violates the "inalienable" right to life guaranteed by the Kansas Constitution. The court conceded the penalty hearing was fraught with errors, but the majority of justices did not believe they impacted the verdict.

On his last day as Kansas attorney general, Derek Schmidt mentioned the recurring court challenges and contended that "the slow but steady march toward justice continues." His comments were reported in January 2023.

5

The Lighter Side

Lest you think everything that happened in Topeka was solemn and gloomy as we worked diligently to serve the people of Kansas, I want to share a few stories that may give you some insight about moments we fondly remember with a smile.

Legislators often took trips to various facilities; one time, I was accompanying the chairman of the Ways and Means Committee to a conference at the University of Kansas in the Student Union. At the conclusion of the day, we were about to leave the Union when the chairman, Senator August "Gus" Bogina, noticed they were showing a film in the theater called *Debbie Does Dallas*. Well, anyone just out of college, like me, was familiar with *Debbie Does Dallas*. I'd been a fraternity man when I saw it.

He insisted he wanted to find out exactly what kind of movies they were showing. Some of us tried to convince Bogina this wasn't a good idea, but he persisted. He approached the cashier in the box office, and she attempted to placate him by insisting it was reserved for students. He quickly identified himself as chairman of the Senate Ways and Means Committee and insisted we were going in one way or another.

Needless to say, there was more loving going on in the Student Union than there was in the parking lot. About thirty minutes into it, the chairman decided to put an end to it and went out to demand that the projectionist stop the film. You might imagine we weren't the most popular guys at the university after that, and we were even written up in the *Uni-*

versity Daily Kansan newspaper for having violated every constitutional right they thought they had.

The manager of the theater ultimately placed a call to the chancellor or to the dean (I can't remember which) wanting to know who we were, why we were there, what right we had to engage the projectionist, and so on. The chairman, for his part, demanded to receive the film, which was produced after he threatened to cut some of the KU budget.

Chairman Bogina took it back to the state Legislature and proceeded to show it to the Ways and Means Committee. Somehow along the way, unsurprisingly, things got leaked. Sure enough, a copy of the film was made, and one day I walked into the Kansas Press Office in the Capitol only to find every reporter huddled around a computer watching *Debbie Does Dallas*.

* * * * *

I enjoyed recently reminiscing with a Senate colleague, Sen. Paul Feliciano, about our birthday dinners over the years. We were both born in March, so we celebrated together, along with our other Senate friends, Democrats and Republicans. A group of us often socialized, including Republican Norman Gaar and Democrat Jack Steineger. We played tennis together, ate dinner together, and generally enjoyed each other's company. I didn't know until recently that Paul's Democratic friends asked him why he socialized so much with me. Paul said he told them, "Because I like him." In an interview in September 2022, Feliciano said he loved the bipartisan camaraderie that grew: "You didn't have the horrible split in the way you do today in the world of politics."

Though the Wichita senator said he didn't believe much in labels, he considered me a moderate Republican, one who could meet people in the middle. That's how I described myself as well, from the beginning of my legislative career. At any rate, Paul loved Asian food, so for our joint birthday gathering, he found Hunan, a Topeka restaurant that served what it called a presidential meal: Peking duck with that great sauce, along with rice, soup, and all the fixings.

We invited four Democrats and four Republicans to the meal, and when we got to the restaurant, I asked to see the cook. Feliciano describes it this way: "Ed Reilly, being Ed Reilly, said, 'I've got to meet the cook,'" who he said was a huge individual. He says I asked if the chef liked whiskey or scotch, and he wanted to know why. As Feliciano remembers it: "[Ed Reilly] said, 'Because I'm going to take care of you if you take care of us. It's a special dinner, a birthday dinner.' So he goes out to his car and pulls out a bottle of Paddy Irish whiskey and brings it to the chef." He and I both remember that the meal was excellent. In fact, from that year on, we all had the same presidential meal for our birthdays. We thought a presidential meal was quite fitting for us state legislators.

I remember a time when we were debating a controversial issue, and the mood had been so tense on the floor we decided it was time to lighten it up. Paul and I knew what we were going to do, and we told Ross Doyen, Senate president. The two of us began exchanging words in front of the Senate; Paul and I often debated issues, but this time we were getting more and more heated. Finally, senators, the press, and other onlookers were sure we were going to get physical. It appeared we were headed for fisticuffs. In fact, Bob Talkington, vice president of the Senate, tackled me (he was a former KU football player) to keep me from attacking Feliciano. Doyen got so mad he broke his gavel. But we stopped, shook hands, and assured all onlookers we were friends. It could have been April Fool's Day, but whatever day it was, everyone broke into laughter. I'm afraid if legislators tried this today in the US Congress, it would develop into a full-fledged riot, just like it did in the pre-Kansas days. There are pictures in the Capitol of legislators standing with rifles in the chambers.

*****

Then there was the time we wanted to socialize, and we went to a beautiful club in Kansas City, Kansas. It was known as a Mafia restaurant boasting several tiers, and there were some crazy things going on. Feliciano recalls, "Ed Reilly was always on point, and he called the waiter over and told him we just wanted to have drinks." So we'd had a few drinks, and it was probably ten thirty or eleven thirty, and the doors opened and the police came in to raid the club. They planned to check the license, I guess, and make sure everyone had proper IDs. There were also some gambling machines in the restaurant. Feliciano remembered I approached the police sergeant leading the raid and told him I had a group of visitors with me, and that we'd come here for a drink. The sergeant said we should get up, leave our drinks on the table, and we shouldn't ask any questions. So we followed him to the back door and left. The police did close the place.

I remember another visit to Gus Fasone's Supper Club in Kansas City, Kansas, but this time it was as much business as pleasure. We were trying to come up with a treaty between Missouri and Kansas concerning the Missouri River, since boundaries had shifted because of erosion. I set up a luncheon and invited committees from Missouri and Kansas to attend. Gus fixed us an elaborate Italian meal, and we sat around the table trying to negotiate a great problem. It was the topic of numerous news stories because no law enforcement agency in Kansas or Missouri wanted to take over in cases when they found bodies on the sandbar by the Missouri River.

The long and the short of it is that after two or three hours, we hadn't gotten anywhere. The Missouri folks wanted to leave, but I said "No, you can't leave. We'll all be embarrassed to go back and say we didn't succeed at anything; we have no resolution of any kind." So I went to Gus, the owner, and asked him to do me a favor: "I want you to bar the doors; put up whatever you have, a chain or whatever, and simultaneously bring in martinis, drinks already mixed up and bring them in." We were in a private dining room. He did, and it worked perfectly. I said, "Gentlemen, we aren't going to leave. We're going to sit and have our drinks and we're going to hammer this out." And by golly, we did! We took that treaty back, and based on what we told our fellow legislators, they approved, and so did the governors. Eventually the treaty had to be approved by the US Congress.

* * * * *

As Paul and I reminisced, we also remembered some pretty wild Saint Patrick's Day parades in Kansas City. One in particular stands out—eight of us took off to have a good time, the Parade Committee made signs for us, and we were treated like royalty. We rented a suite at the Muehlebach Hotel, and we had a great time. Feliciano remembered that at one point I handed him my car keys and said, "You're the designated driver. Don't drink any more." He didn't, but that didn't faze the rest of us, and we quite enjoyed that Saint Patrick's Day.

Another Saint Patrick's Day also stands out in my memory. Senators Barr, Garr, Steineger and I sponsored a Saint Patrick's Day party in Topeka for several years, a function that became known as one of the most entertaining parties during a legislative session. This was possible through the generosity of Hallmark Cards, which furnished most of the décor, and the Ramada Inn of Topeka, which offered its popular pub on the lower level.

Well attended, the party often attracted the governor and staff as well as members of the Senate and House. Governor Bob Docking, who always enjoyed a good time, attended one we all remember. It was going well, until suddenly a group of young guys started coming in that no one recognized. Then we saw one of them confronting Governor Docking about a pending legislative issue. Apparently, it was one he was willing to fight about.

In an attempt to resolve the matter, we politely asked this guy—who we'd realized was from some fraternity—to leave. At that point, a literal riot began. I was pushed, and Governor Docking was ready to fight. His one-man security officer from the Kansas Highway Patrol was fast on his feet, scuttling the governor out a lower entrance while the Topeka police department entered. They came with two police dogs and whistles to end the riot, and it did promptly.

Turns out, the young men—who were on a pledge brother walk from a university from another state—were escorted out and, to my knowledge, questioned and released. That was the last Saint Patrick's party we ever had, and it's still one to talk about all these years later.

Chapter 5

* * * * *

Who doesn't like to ride in a limousine? That was my thought when Ford dealer Danny Zeck and I started talking about opening a limousine service in Leavenworth. We called it Executive Limousine Service. Our first car was a Lincoln limousine Danny managed to find that had a few miles on it. It was on their showroom floor, and we had a grand opening, with champagne and all the hoopla that goes with it.

Later on, a group of senators and our Leavenworth County sheriff decided to try a similar business, figuring it could both make money and be fun. So I, along with Senators Jack Steineger and Norman Garr and a good friend, Sheriff Terry Campbell, decided to buy a stretch limo that was a couple of years old, and form a corporation. We called it JENTs, using the initials of our first names.

Terry liked to help get jobs for inmates released from jail, assuming they'd committed fairly minor offenses and had maintained a good record in jail. A guy named Warren Harris was ready for release, so Terry arranged for him to be a part-time janitor in the sheriff's department and made arrangements for him to get a chauffeur's license so he could drive the limousine as needed. A receptionist at the Reilly Agency scheduled appointments, and we'd call Wayne, whose nickname was Red, so he could pick up the customer. Sometimes it would be taking someone to or from the airport, sometimes it was someone going out for the evening.

A lot of times we'd use it for ourselves. Steineger, for example, went to school with actor Ed Asner, best known as "Lou Grant" in the TV program *The Mary Tyler Moore Show*. When Asner came to Kansas City, which he did pretty often, Jack would use the limo to pick him up and take him around town. Terry remembered him as a "nice gentleman, funnier than heck with a quick wit," in an interview in July 2022.

I used the limousine service when dignitaries were in Topeka, and Terry used it too, when he was teaching classes for the Justice Department in the Kansas City area. When judges, county attorneys and others who taught with him were in town, they wanted to see attractions like the Truman Library and the Chiefs stadium. We were also generous and charged reduced prices when friends wanted to rent it for a kid's prom or some other special event.

We made enough money to keep the limo gassed up and insured, but not much more, so it was far from the moneymaker we'd planned. That was one reason I wanted to get out of the business. But there was an even more urgent reason for me to get out. One of the drivers called me; I think he was a military guy. It could be he just wanted me to know, but the car had a window that went up between the seats. It also had a monitor so the customer in back could buzz the driver, and he would open the channel. One night the channel was open, and he could hear sexual activity going on and smell marijuana smoke—so that was the last of our business venture.

* * * * *

You never knew what adventures could arise when Gaar, Steineger, and I were together. The three of us shared a memorable visit in 1974 to Vail, Colorado, where we had the opportunity to ski with President Gerald Ford on Vail Mountain. It was especially exciting to be going down the mountain with the Secret Service agents accompanying Ford, who were carrying automatic weapons over their shoulders. The only thing we missed was the chance to sit with him in the hot tub after a hard day of skiing.

The friendships with those two Senate buddies stood the test of time and distance. Steineger kept a forty-foot sailboat at Red Hook Harbor in St. Thomas, and we often sailed there. Once I was in the Department of Justice as president of the Parole Commission, I handed out hats to my colleagues that read "Commissioner, US Parole Commission."

We had those hats on when we went into a bar in Red Hook. A couple of days later, we went to that same bar, but this time the owner had a request. "Do me a favor," he said. "When you come in here, take those hats off. Don't wear those hats here. You're scaring away my customers." Those customers were ones heavily involved in the drug trade, so I guess it's no wonder he was losing business.

6

Life Experiences

Being a victim can make us feel violated and vulnerable, but it's also a life experience many of us endure. I was a teenager the first time I witnessed it. My sister Mary Ann was suffering from mononucleosis, and she was resting in the master bedroom on the first floor of our home on Broadway. I happened to be there when she realized someone was peeping into her bedroom window. I took a gun with me when I went outside, because I wanted to scare the guy.

I was hiding in the driveway of our neighbor, Bud Heinz, and I could hear our Saint Bernard, Mike, chasing the peeper. Mike was so big he couldn't catch the guy, who by that time was jogging. He jogged past his car, then turned around and came back to the car and got in. By that time, I approached the car with my gun.

That's when the police got there. They all knew me, and they said, "Ed, put down that gun." They handcuffed him, and I sure threw that gun right down. It turns out he was a member of the Junior Chamber of Commerce. He could have been the president, I'm not sure. A neighbor who came by recognized him spread-eagled on the ground.

The next memorable victim-related event our family experienced was a bank robbery in Lansing on June 30, 1970. My father and I had founded the First State Bank in Lansing with several other investors in the mid-1960s, as the community's previous bank had gone under. The robbers probably didn't know what hit them, as not only local law enforcement but also Federal Bureau of Investigation agents quickly responded to the scene. According to an account in the July 1, 1970, edition of *The Leavenworth Times*, two of the three Kansas City, Kansas, men who robbed it were immediately turned over to the FBI. Sheriff Dan Hawes said the third man, who was wounded, was initially hospitalized at Cushing Hospital.

Coincidentally, but luckily for us, the FBI was in town for training in the Federal Magistrate Court chambers in the top floor of the Leavenworth Post Office. That was in addition to Lansing police, the Leavenworth County Sheriff's Department, the Kansas Highway Patrol, and even Kansas State Penitentiary. A deputy warden at KSP brought a canister of pepper gas to the Lansing police, who dispensed it from the roof into the bank.

The Times reported that the men inadvertently tripped a silent alarm at the bank, which rang at the sheriff's office and brought a small army of law officers sweeping in for the arrest. Hawes identified the robbers as Jessie James Quinn, twenty-four; and Reginald Kelsey, twenty-one; both of whom had appeared before a federal judge on arraignment. The third man, treated at Cushing and turned over to law enforcement, was identified as Wilson Caldwell, twenty-eight. He was then detained at the Wyandotte County Jail.

Two of the robbers were still in the bank when officers arrived, within minutes after the alarm sounded. Caldwell was shot in the left hip by Deputy Robert Dougherty when he ran from the door on the side of the bank. Kelsey and Quinn remained in the bank, until the pepper gas—stronger than tear gas—flushed them out, according to *The Times*.

A teller at the bank told law enforcement two men entered the door around noon on June 30 and wanted to buy traveler's checks. She didn't know how to issue them, so she turned them over to the other teller. Two shorter men immediately entered the bank, one pulling a gun on the two women while the other brandished a weapon on the executive vice president. They forced the two women to crouch on the floor with their heads down, yelling not to look at them, *The Times* reported. None of the robbers wore masks.

One of the robbers was in the dropped ceiling when law enforcement arrived, and he was gassed. Another one surrendered. Deputy Sheriff Robert Dougherty was driving by the bank when he got the call, as the bank's alarm had gone off. The third robber had started shooting from the inside, and when he ran from the bank, Dougherty saw him and drove the patrol car over the curb, reached out of his window and started shooting, hitting him in the hip. So all three were captured, and they didn't get any money. But the bank administrator, who we all knew had a drinking problem, was still inside when the bank was gassed, and he quit, saying that was enough for him.

* * * * *

On October 1, 1979, an unbelievable scenario played out at the Reilly & Sons Agency, then located at Fifth and Delaware streets. It started out like any other morning as the clerical staff, including office manager and ten-year employee Nancy Metz, came to work around 8:00 a.m. Ann Foster, one of the staff members, recalled in an August 2022 interview that she was sitting at one of the four desks in the front of the office. Her desk was behind the one next to Nancy's. One of the women, a good friend of thirty-six-year-old Nancy, was at a doctor's appointment, but the other three were there. So was my brother Jerry, who was in his office; it had glass windows, but they were draped, so he couldn't see what was happening in the main part of the office. Dave Nunn, also part of the staff, was sitting at a desk further back.

Ann recalls that around 8:30 a.m., Nancy got a phone call. She spoke briefly and when she hung up, she said, "Oh, my God, Ross [her ex-husband Ross McReady] is here and wants to take Kim [their daughter, a student at West Junior High] out of school to go home with him to Texas." She told him "Absolutely not."

Nancy didn't tell Jerry what had happened. McReady apparently went to the school, where officials wouldn't let him take Kim. He immediately drove to Reilly's and walked through the door on the Delaware side. Ann said not many people entered that front door; most entered the door on the Fifth Street side. But he walked in, and she was facing him. She remembers he was wearing a "fall-like plaid shirt and jeans," and he walked straight up to Nancy's desk. "Why wouldn't you let me take her?" he asked her, but the only word she got out was "But…" The next thing Ann remembers is the first gunshot. He didn't give Nancy a chance to speak before shooting her in the head. He shot her in the chest next, and she fell on the floor.

"It took me a little while," Ann said, "but I could smell the gunpowder. At first I thought someone was shooting outside through the windows." When she realized he was inside shooting, she fell to the floor and crawled underneath her desk. "I didn't have anywhere to go," Ann said. "I think if I'd got up and tried to go to the basement door, he would have shot me. The girl who sat in front of Nancy was right in front of the basement door, and she ran to the basement."

By the time Jerry realized what was going on, McReady had walked around and shot Nancy four more times in the head, Ann recalls. "He kept shooting her. I counted the bullets. That was the Larry in me [her husband Larry was a Kansas Highway Patrolman]. He carried the same gun, a .357. I knew one bullet was left in the gun."

McReady walked to the middle of the aisle and challenged them. "Are there any heroes in here?"

"I didn't make a peep," Ann said. "Dave [Nunn] had already run into Mr. Reilly's way back office." She learned later Jerry was getting his gun out of his desk. "I was real quiet. I heard the last shot. I thought he either shot Jerry or Dave or he shot himself."

She crawled across the floor so she could see he'd shot himself in the head. At that point Jerry was out of his office, gun in hand. By that time Leavenworth Police Officer Bill Klingele ran into the office. A lady who worked in the shoe store next door heard the shots and called 911. It turned out Klingele was only a block away.

"Bill had his gun drawn," Ann remembers. "He said to Jerry, 'Drop the gun.'" After he did, Jerry helped Ann up and Klingele came into the office. Ray Graf, who worked at Leavenworth National Bank, ran in as well. Jerry had been on the phone with him, and he'd dropped the phone and started running toward the Reilly office, which was just up the block.

Ann had run out the front door by that time, and Ray "caught me when I started going down the steps." Jerry was outside, too, by then. Her first instinct was to run around the corner and go in the side door. "I could see everything," she said. "Jerry immediately grabbed me and put my head down and said, 'Don't come back in.' But I'd already seen her. It was too late. I guess I was in shock by that time, but I wished I'd never gone in that way. It turned out to be a nightmare."

Her husband Larry's boss, the highway patrol colonel, called him to say he needed to be home with Ann the rest of the day.

"Ed was in Ireland when it happened, but Jerry got him on the phone right away and filled him in, and he came home right away," Ann said.

Nancy had divorced McReady about eight years earlier, Ann remembers, and she'd married her second husband, John Metz, in April 1974. John Metz was working at Fort Leavenworth, and Nancy called him as soon as she hung up with McReady. She'd told him, "He's in town and he's trying to take Kim." Metz went to their home on Twentieth Street before going to the Reilly office and got a shotgun.

Ann remembers John running across the street with that gun. "Terry Campbell was sheriff at the time," she said, and Terry told him, "It's too late." Ann said they didn't let Metz inside, and she was glad that he didn't have to see Nancy that way.

After their divorce, Ann said, Nancy let McReady raise their son, who turned out to be exactly like his father. "He was a gun person. They shot animals, like cats. He followed in his father's footsteps."

Ann remembers when the son was eighteen, he wanted to see his mother, and she and John let him stay at their home. "She came to work and said, 'He carries a gun. There is a gun in his room.'" She and her husband started locking their door at night. When he went home to Texas, the son apparently gave his father a map of every room in their house, the school, and the Reilly office, which they found in his truck.

Ann said they all speculated McReady came to Leavenworth to shoot the entire family, because he went to the Metz home first, but nobody was there. She recalled he had an arsenal of guns in his truck. According to an October 2, 1979, story in *The Leavenworth Times,* when police checked his truck, they found a .22 caliber automatic long rifle, an automatic pistol, a Winchester rifle, and a container of ammunition, among other items.

The day of Nancy's funeral, office staff was "all freaked out," because the son came to the service, Ann remembers. But police surrounded him the entire time and didn't take their eyes off him.

Ann occasionally saw the daughter, Kim, through the years, and she recalls Kim saying her brother had moved to Las Vegas and ended up killing himself. She'd severed all ties with him, but apparently he still had her listed as his sister, and police had contacted her when he committed suicide.

Nancy was obviously afraid of her ex-husband, Ann believes. "Like Jerry said, if she'd said something when he called, since she was already afraid of him, we could have had police there. We could have gone in the safe and locked the door. He said he could have protected all of us."

I was skeptical Jerry could have really protected them, since McReady seemed bound to kill his ex-wife. I think if he had been unsuccessful that day, he would have tried again.

* * * * *

When I accepted my appointment as chairman of the US Parole Commission from President George H. W. Bush, with the backing of Senators Bob Dole and Nancy Kassebaum, I realized if someone was displeased with a parole decision, violence could occur. Such was the case in December 1993, after Leonard Peltier's first parole hearing.

Peltier, a Native American activist and member of the American Indian Movement, was one of the high-profile inmates incarcerated at the US Penitentiary at Leavenworth, transferred there from US Lompoc—a low-security federal correctional facility in California—in 1985. He was serving two life sentences for convictions of killing two FBI agents on the Pine Ridge reservation in South Dakota. The case was highly publicized and attracted the attention of Hollywood actors such as Robert Redford and Barbra Streisand, and many others, who advocated for Peltier's parole. Many people showed up at the hearings to support him, and numerous walkers and protestors banded in front of the US Penitentiary on his behalf.

On a Monday, the parole examiner conducted Mr. Peltier's hearing, and I denied his release. In the early morning hours of the Friday that same week, my Leavenworth home on Broadway was firebombed. Someone had entered the side gate and stood close to the window of a glassed-in porch and hurled a Molotov cocktail inside. Thankfully, I was not in the house, and first responders were able to extinguish the fire. Although the floor was carpeted, there was cement underneath, preventing the house from burning down. If the perpetrator had moved over ten feet, it would have hit the living room, and the house would have been destroyed. Fortunately, the Leavenworth Police and Fire departments' response was rapid.

Although the Federal Bureau of Investigation, the Bureau of Alcohol, Tobacco and Firearms, and the Leavenworth Police could not conclude who threw the firebomb, I'm convinced it was in response to the Leonard Peltier case. In 2005, Peltier was transferred to the Lewisburg, PA, maximum security penitentiary. He remained there until 2011, when he went to a maximum security prison in Florida. President Joe Biden commuted Peltier's life sentence on January 20, 2025. He was released to home confinement the following month and is now on the Turtle Mountain Reservation in North Dakota.

* * * * *

That firebombing incident made me even more aware there was always the possibility of being killed, as a commissioner and decision-maker, since the killer might see that as a way of resolving problems. There's no question I and the other members of the Parole Commission were often in danger, and so were the victims' relatives. Some reported being stalked by those who had harmed their family members. I concluded that many who commit these horrendous crimes have no conscience, and anything goes to fulfill whatever desire they might have. Though we may try to find reasons for their conduct, I believe there are just some who aren't valuable members of society, and they can't live peacefully with those who are.

The firebombing was the first major assault I endured in my career with the criminal justice system, though prior to this event, I'd received threats from inmates serving time in the Kansas prison system. These inmates likely didn't care for my position on punishment for their crimes. Since I was an advocate and legislator who had to argue various issues before the Kansas Senate, my views were public and published.

During my tenure on the US Parole Commission, some exciting events occurred in our office. One was a major bomb scare, when a package arrived that had all the elements of a bomb. When X-rayed through our scanner, what showed up was a leaky package and some wires, which fit the definition of a bomb. The bomb squad arrived, only to discover it was a false alarm when they exploded the package with high-velocity water cannons.

Mike Gaines, President Bill Clinton's appointee as commissioner and later chairman, recalls that day as well. In an August 2023 interview, he mentioned the equipment that staff used to screen mail, similar to the setup at an airport, and the one using it came running to ask, "Will you come look at the box?" On the image you could see two tubes that looked like dynamite—if you're looking for a bomb, everything looks suspicious. Then you could see a big round cylinder-looking thing that the X-ray couldn't penetrate. There was also a long rectangular box and odds and ends.

Gaines continued:

We had the Department of Justice security look at it, and they contacted the DOJ bomb people and evacuated our floor of the building. The bomb group came in with these Hazmat-looking uniforms, with a high-pressure water cannon. We were all outside, and they took it to the hallway and used the cannon to blow it up. It actually was a care package a mother was trying to send to her son in prison. The two tubes were a package of Oreos, the cylinder was a jar of peanut butter, the rectangular box was a carton of cigarettes, and the odds and ends were packages of sugar and artificial sweetener.

"It was the biggest mess," Gaines added, noting that the hallway was covered with embossed wallpaper. He figures the wallpaper still has bits of Oreos and peanut butter in it, unless they've since repapered.

Needless to say, the building's office routine was totally disrupted that day. The structure, which is in Chevy Chase, Maryland, also housed many doctors and professional associations as well as a surgical center. Patients undergoing surgery were carried from the building on gurneys.

Since our office wasn't in a government building, we weren't subject to security screening to enter. We had a visitor one day who scared the hell out of most of our staff. He mentioned the name of an offender, Brett Kimberlin, and said he came to interrogate a commissioner as to why he hadn't been paroled earlier. Kimberlin was a convicted drug smuggler serving time at a federal penitentiary in Oklahoma. During the 1988 presidential campaign, Kimberlin had alleged that Republican vice-presidential nominee Dan Quayle had purchased marijuana from him in the early 1970s. Fortunately, it didn't lead to a terrible situation, but it was an event that seldom happened at our offices despite our lack of security. Other than locked doors and a camera, everyone came freely if they knew the door combination.

I shall never forget the day of 9/11, when most of the commissioners and staff were present and I was monitoring my TV, which I did many mornings. I heard the news when the first plane struck the World Trade Center. When they announced a second plane had hit the Twin Towers, it became obvious to me we were under some sort of attack. The phones were ringing on our desks to advise that we needed to evacuate to a site near Rockville, Maryland, and await further instructions. No one really took the advice seriously, including me, but I did feel the need to get home to my nine-year-old son and his caregiver, who were just three miles from the office.

I instructed the rest of the staff to rush to their families and to pray on the way. The tragedy of that day stays with us all as we reflect on the deaths of our fellow Americans. Within seven days of the attack, I had the opportunity to travel to Pennsylvania to observe the remains of the plane that passengers successfully diverted; the terrorists crashed that plane head-on into the ground after passengers started breaking into the cockpit. It was an eerie sight to be there so shortly afterward and smell the burning flesh. The tail of the plane was still smoking, and the fire continued to burn fuel. I accompanied Marjorie Ackerman, regional director for the Red Cross, to the site, as she had asked me to go with her. She was also an ordained minister and a chaplain in several hospitals.

I believe some passengers bravely sacrificed themselves, realizing what was happening. That is true love: when you give your own life for the sake of others. Today, we can only hope and pray that those days will not return to America, and the current hostility and lack of respect for others won't result in such actions. It often takes a tragedy like 9/11 to bring us to our knees, but unfortunately, that only lasted for a short time. How soon we forget. But there may be another time when we're prepared to make the kind of sacrifice those who perished made.

Americans still have a lot of growing up to do if we're going to return to a climate of respect and gratitude for our great nation. We need to remember those who have fought and died to preserve the liberty many take for granted. Serving for more than seventeen years at the federal level definitely qualified me for another bachelor's degree in humanity.

* * * * *

Another totally unexpected incident occurred in the office on Father's Day 2006. My office was broken into, and personal documents relating to the commission were copied. I knew this thanks to an astute, loyal, and dedicated personal secretary who had been with the commission for many years. She was wise enough to notice on the following Monday morning that documents from my desk were now on the bottom shelf of our massive copy machine. When she approached me with the copies, I was taken aback since I hadn't made them. They'd been copied from a spiral notebook with pages numbered so they couldn't be extracted. As a result, you would know they were missing.

It was obvious from the discovery that someone had entered my loft office over the previous weekend and copied pages in the notebook I used to retain notes on conversations with various agency directors and appointees. Needless to say, we were shocked to think that someone gained access to a commissioner's locked office. My alert assistant and an examiner had unexpectedly showed up for some office work time and surprised the intruders. In their haste, they forgot certain pages from the documents they'd been copying.

I immediately informed my colleagues about what had happened. Then I visited the Justice Department and requested that the Office of the Inspector General investigate the incident. The agency launched a lengthy probe—unfortunate for the commission, because agents from the Office of the Inspector General conducted many interviews. The investigation continued for months and concluded that indeed, from all indications, two people had surreptitiously and unlawfully entered my office. This was troubling news because the US Parole Commission is a unique institution charged with dispensing the most important decisions on fellow human beings who are incarcerated. The inmates' families, if they are fortunate enough to have a family, anguish daily over the fate of loved ones, who in most cases just want to serve their time and get on with their life.

* * * * *

Another life experience didn't involve me or my family being victims, but it did occur in my neighborhood on Broadway in Leavenworth. That was the rescue of David Lozenski from his burning home with the help of Rick Schneider, my campaign manager for many years. Rick lived across the street from the Lozenski residence.

On September 22, 1990, I was taking my morning jog when I noticed flames shooting from a window of the first floor of the house on South Broadway. Entering, I heard Mrs. Lozenski screaming that she was trying to move David to safety in a wheelchair. The house, and the entire area, were filled with intense, black smoke, but Rick and I were able to get into the hallway and discovered the nineteen-year-old boy's wheelchair stuck in a hallway.

By removing him from the wheelchair, we were able to get him into the backyard, and his mother followed us. About that time, the Leavenworth Fire Department arrived and began to extinguish the fire. That was my first personal experience with Leavenworth County's Emergency Medical Services. Rick and I needed oxygen since we'd inhaled a great deal of the heavy, black smoke associated with burning furniture and carpet. The fire had started in the living room.

I really wasn't thinking of my own safety when I entered that house. When you get into situations like that, the adrenaline starts pumping and you just realize someone needs help. Afterwards, you really get emotional and think of what could have happened.

Rick and I weren't expecting to be treated as heroes, so we were surprised when we were nominated for the Carnegie Medal for Heroism, which we received the following May. In my opinion, saving another's life was just the right thing to do. Nevertheless, we appreciated the recognition.

The Lozenski family of eight children and I grew up on South Broadway in Leavenworth, Kansas. Many of them who were classmates of mine still live there. Growing up in a town where I know so many of the residents is a life many children no longer enjoy in our mobile society. That teaches you what life is all about, how much a person can endure, and how people react. I believe this kind of life helped me deal with the situations I encountered as a public servant.

I believe it's made me compassionate toward the misfortunes and mistakes of others. With our lives comes responsibility—responsibility for others, responsibility for ourselves, and a need to be considerate of others. In so doing, we are paying back some of the "rent" we owe on the earthly space we occupy.

I've never held myself out as someone who is better than anyone else or whose fortune has been better than others, and I think this will be corroborated by those who know me. I've tried to convey that during my public service and in business. I think my deep-seated egalitarian feeling helped catapult me into the Kansas Legislature and later to my federal appointment. I also must credit the help and support of a long-standing friend, Senator Bob Dole, and our Kansas delegation.

7

Our Love Story

For an Irishman who's been a bachelor until fifty, it's extremely difficult to say "I do," unless you're with an extremely delicious model who has enticed you into a commitment you never dreamed you'd fall for. Well, Ms. Slattery was not of that variety, but our storied courtship is one for the books. During our ten-year relationship, I hadn't been able to make that commitment. Finally, her father, Charles Slattery, had had enough—during a holiday celebration, he called me to the pantry in my future wife's lovely home outside Atchison, in the community of Good Intent.

He opened the cupboard and pulled out a jug of Old Crow bourbon, and he poured me a full glass. Now, I like my whiskey, but not in a water glass with no ice or water to spare. But it was obvious there was no way I was leaving that room until he made his Irish wishes known. Even after that session, it took me six months to finally get around to proposing at my parish church, Sacred Heart, after a New Year's Eve Mass. My family attended, hiding in the back of the church after the service; they were aware of what I was about to do, but they didn't believe it would happen. Neither did Father Jerry Sheeds, who volunteered to have his dog witness the affair if we did it right then and there.

* * * * *

I believe most of us men with Irish backgrounds are never quite sure what we're looking for in a lady with whom to share our lives. I was no exception, and I believe my mother and father would have never believed that when I finally said "I do" it would be with the real love of my life. Like most guys, I'd had many loves in my bachelor years whom I still remember and respect. But in 1974, my bachelor life and playboy reputation took a big turn.

At the time, I was serving in the Kansas Senate, but I was also a candidate for US Congress in the Second District. That's when a Democratic colleague in the Kansas House, Jim Slattery, introduced me to his sister Luci. I had known Jim for quite a while before he was in the Legislature. He recently recalled our meeting in 1967. "I was eighteen and a cub teletyper when I first met Ed in the State House," Jim said. "He made quite an impression and had good rapport with the press. It was later I thought my sister needed to meet this dude."

As we chatted, Jim reminded me of everything that was going on in politics during those years. As one of the youngest members of the Kansas Senate, I was eyeing the political landscape to see where I might fit in 1974, the next election cycle. Since I had been elected to the Kansas House and then the Senate at such a young age, I felt indispensable.

At that time there was a lot of controversy about the Second District US Congressman, Dr. Bill Roy, a Topeka Democrat whose reputation for performing abortions became an issue in his race for reelection. The wolves were at his doorstep, and 1974 sounded like a time for me to think about a congressional race, which a few friends in the political arena were suggesting. As an elected senator, I wouldn't have to give up my seat if I lost, so I announced.

But then there was another shocker: Roy decided to take on US Senator Bob Dole, of all people. I ended up with a primary challenge from John Peterson, a former House member from Topeka, who lost to Democrat Martha Keys, 55 percent to 43.9 percent. She served from 1975–1979 and then lost her seat to Jim Jeffries, a Republican from Atchison, who served from 1979–1983.

I gladly returned to my job of representing the people in my district and decided the national scene effort was a great experience but far too expensive; today it makes no sense at all when you examine what it costs to run for the House or Senate. Jeffries was challenged and defeated by my brother-in-law, Democrat Jim Slattery, who served from 1983–1995.

It was definitely a wild time, with Senator Bob Dole barely reelected in one of the closet races of his life. In the course of my later service on the Parole Commission, I had the opportunity to see Martha Keys on a number of occasions. We had a chance to have a more intimate visit about what might have been the result if I'd won the nomination.

But 1974 turned out to be a highlight in my life despite the campaign. Attending the wedding of Jim Slattery and Linda Smith that year was truly significant. I was introduced to Jim's sister Luci, who was a bridesmaid, and the rest is history.

Jim's invitation to his wedding created a dramatic turn in the direction of my life. Luci was a typical Irish lady with Slattery ancestors on both sides of her family, including her father Charles and mother Rose O'Connor. She radiated an exuberance and love of life that no sensible man could ignore, especially this Irishman.

I'd been to Ireland, home of our third-generation ancestors, many times looking for the perfect Luci. I had a number of Irish loves who were beautiful, passionate, and thoughtful who also could not be ignored, but I recognized late that it's difficult to displace someone from their homeland and their culture. Besides, someone else was destined to be my soulmate.

So looking back, Luci was a real find that I couldn't pass up. We began dating in 1974. Since the Slatterys lived in the community of Good Intent, it was only a twenty-five-minute trip to the Slattery farm, and I was burning up the highway as I beat my way to Luci's door.

I loved the warmth of her mother Rose and father Charles, particularly when Rose offered me some of her homemade pie or Charles took me in the kitchen pantry for a shot of Old Crow bourbon. Spending time with the Slattery family and Luci's two brothers, Mike and Jim and their families, was like coming home to a second family.

My first serious date with Luci was in Kansas City, Kansas, where she was teaching. I arrived in my white buck shoes, white belt, and as a Leavenworth County reserve deputy sheriff, with a pistol in the glove compartment. When Luci saw all this, I could tell she was overwhelmed. Afterwards, she asked her brother Jim, "Why would you think I would go out with a guy who has white shoes and belt and carries a weapon?"

Ironically enough, a little later in our relationship, she came to appreciate that pistol-packing cowboy from Leavenworth. During my congressional campaign, Luci and her cousin from Kansas City, Kansas, were on the run to appeal to Wyandotte County voters. They ended up in the city late at night, and while they were stopped at a light, four young men who looked pretty threatening approached the car. Luci, realizing that the pistol-packing senator had a revolver in the glove compartment, quickly retrieved it. She casually waved it at the guys, who she reported promptly took off.

That was just another of the interesting experiences she had campaigning for this GOP candidate. Her friends frequently asked her why she was working for a Republican. She had a prompt comeback: "There are good Republicans and Democrats as well as bad." Her experience as a teacher and working for her brother, Jim, taught her about the grassroots of politics and how to capture the hearts of those she talked to.

But back to our love story—the long and short of it was that we got over the hump and began to see one another on a steady basis. The sad part of the story is that it took me from 1974 until 1986 before I had the good sense to propose to her. But the six months between that fateful meeting with her father in the pantry and the New Year's Eve when I proposed gave us a chance to talk out many issues that we'd never spoken candidly about, and we gained a better understanding of what both of us wanted out of life.

We recognized she had a career as a well-known teacher, and I was still working in the insurance and real estate firm and serving in public office. And we'd be marrying into a mixed family. Luci and her family were strong Democrats. My family was a hybrid as my father was a staunch Republican and my mother was a Kansas City, MO, Democrat.

We knew we could overcome those differences and focus on what we wanted out of life and how to help others reach their goals.

Luci had a reputation as one of the finest and most eloquent teachers in the Atchison system; to this day, when some of her former students recognize me as the lucky gent who captured her, they come up and express their love and gratitude for how she inspired them. I hope someday folks will come up to my son and family and express that sentiment for this geezer.

Luci and I were married at Sacred Heart Church on May 16, 1986, in Leavenworth, and some referred to it as a "wedding from Camelot." I wouldn't, in my humility, go that far, but it was certainly impressive in that many folks came to watch outside the church and wish us the best with applause and even some flowers. I vividly remember walking down the aisle, as Luci picked the roses from the containers she'd planned for each pew and handed them to all the ladies. All the while, Roxie Whittaker and her choir members sang "Reach Out and Touch." It was a tear-jerking moment for me as well as a lot of assembled friends.

Sheriff Terry Campbell always seemed to be around when needed and he remains a dear friend. He'd arranged all the escorts—police and sheriff's officers delivered the wedding party to the Fort Leavenworth Officers' Club in a timely fashion. He used the Army ROTC cadets of Leavenworth High School to drive golf carts so those needing a lift to the reception and some who needed to leave could make it to their vehicles.

All this organization allowed the bride and groom to welcome some 2,000 guests taking over the entire club. Two bands provided tunes for dancing, and the club's great staff prepared a buffet table fit for a king and queen. On hand was a fellow so important in our lives, Hector Hugo Gavilan and his wife, Margarita, who had previously worked at the fort for the club and commandant.

As always Hector made sure everything was perfect, as did my sister Mary Ann, and Charla, the wife of my best man and brother Jerry. They were all right in the mix to pull it together. You have to remember, they had a lot of time to think about this event they thought would never happen.

In the Sunday edition of *The Leavenworth Times*, May 18, the cutline of a photograph showing Luci and me enjoying our first dance read, "In what many regarded as the social event of the year, state Sen. Edward F. Reilly Jr. of Leavenworth and the former Luci Slattery of Atchison were united in marriage Friday night at Sacred Heart Church."

In the June 1, 1986, edition of the local newspaper, nearly every detail of our ceremony was featured in a story, including Luci's gown, described as a "formal-length gown designed by Frank Masandrea of New York and made of imported white silk taffeta. It was fashioned with a natural bodice, trimmed with beaded alencon lace, irridescents and pearls throughout." The story detailed her jewelry, which included a cluster of diamonds for earrings and a gold watch, my gift to my bride. It even mentioned what I wore—a "Spencer black tuxedo with pleated white wing collar shirt, satin bow tie and cummerbund."

To cap off the wedding and the beginning of our lives, the general at Fort Leavenworth arranged for us to spend our first night of marriage in the home of General George Custer, who served and trained at the fort. The residence is a gorgeous brick three-story home located behind the commanding general's residence, staffed with someone to serve coffee and juice in the morning. We spent our first night of marriage in a king-size bed with crystal chandeliers over our heads. We were honored to have this opportunity, as this home is reserved for dignitaries like the secretary of the Army and even the president of the United States.

The next morning, when I opened the door to coffee and pastries and some fine Irish whiskey, I found a note from a colleague who was in a room above ours. It read: "Wishing you both all the best life can offer and praying last night was not your last stand!" Remember we were in the home of General George W. Custer, who fought the Indians in the battle of the Little Bighorn.

It was not.

Early the next morning, Luci and I departed for the local Elks Club for a breakfast brunch for the wedding party and guests from Ireland. Dr. Eamon and Marlish McDwyer from Ireland made the trip for the rehearsal dinner and wedding, along with Brenda and Jim Elliott—all dear friends from Cavan County, where the Reillys come from. For the next few days, we partied in Kansas City with those who wanted to keep us from consummating the wedding. Little did they know, we already had. We had already decided we should forget running off on a honeymoon when we had friends willing to party with us. It was well worth it and resulted in great memories of a great year in our lives.

It was the beginning of a marvelous marriage supported by our family and friends. Travels later took us to visit relatives and great friends who had been at the fort for studies at the Command and General Staff College. We even took a trip to Cancún. Now having this great sacrament that binds two people into one, it was off to create what we both desired—a child or two to bless our union and fulfill our marriage, even if it was a bit late in life.

Looking back on all of this, as Luci is no longer with me, I have so many wonderful memories to carry me on until my last day, when I can join her and the members of our families in the Kingdom greater than the one in which we have lived and been so fortunate. The woman who was part of my life in raising Joseph after Luci passed always told me to seek help from the Bible, which is all the leadership guide you need. Frankly, I didn't believe her until she shared the version on leadership which put things into perspective; if you were to read it daily, it would be the road map for most every day of your life.

This is the account of our wedding from the June 1, 1986, edition of *The Leavenworth Times*.

Wedding bells ring…
Sen. Reilly marries Luci Slattery
Luci Marie Slattery, daughter of Mrs. Charles Slattery, Atchison, and State Sen. Edward F. Reilly Jr., Leavenworth, son of the late Marian C. and Edward F. Reilly Sr., exchanged wedding vows at a candlelight ceremony the evening of May 16 in Sacred Heart Catholic Church. Miss Slattery is also the daughter of the late Charles B. Slattery.

Father Jerry Sheeds conducted the Roman Catholic High Mass. Other celebrants included Father Angelius Lingenfelser, Father Daniel O'Shea, Father Edwin Watson, Father Bruce Lardie, Father Bill Haegelin, Father Vince Krische, Father Paul Welch, Father Tom Culhane, Father John Stitz and Father Timothy Burke.

Readings were given by the US Representative James C. Slattery, D-Kansas, brother of the bride, Paudie O'Connor, former mayor of Killarney, Ireland, and Dr. Eamon McDwyer, Ireland. The lector was Normand P. Heon. Servers for the Mass were Patrick Sean Slattery, nephew of the bride, and Christopher Randolph Hunter. Readings of gratitude were read by nieces of the couple, Michelle Therese Slattery, Kathleen Sullivan Reilly, and Shannon Sullivan Hewitt.

The mother of the bride wore a mauve formal-length gown with chiffon overlay and was escorted by two of her grandchildren, Erin Maureen Slattery and Sean Francis Slattery. Mrs. Slattery wore a double gardenia corsage with stephanotis.

Entering to "Ode to Joy" played by Lester D. Dalton on the organ and Dr. Roger Stoner on the trumpet, the bride was escorted to the altar by her brother, Michael J. Slattery. She chose a formal-length gown designed by Frank Masandrea of New York and made of imported white silk taffeta. It was fashioned with a natural bodice, trimmed with beaded alencon lace, irridescents and pearls throughout. The contemporary styling featured a high collar neckline, long Juliet sleeves and gathered silk ruffle trim gracing the front and the back of the gown forming a slender basque waist. The full gathered skirt swept into a cathedral-length train. The bride wore a cathedral-length veil of white silk illusion held in place by a satin covered Cleopatra headpiece entirely covered with pearls and silver bugle beads, an original design of Robert Legere. The bridal bouquet was a floor-length cascading arrangement featuring gardenias, sprays of dendrobium orchids and the greenery selected was springeri and pittostorum. Strands of pearls were draped throughout the bouquet. The bride wore a cluster of diamonds for earrings and a gold watch, a gift of the groom.

Serving as matron of honor was Linda Smith Slattery, sister-in-law of the bride. She wore a sapphire blue imported silk taffeta gown featuring a full ruffled scooped neckline and cummerbund waist. Adorning her hair was a comb flyaway veil with silk flowers, silver and white ornamentation and pearl sprays, original designs of the bride and Cathy K. Highley. She wore a single strand of pearls and matching pearl earrings.

The other honor attendants, dressed identically to the matron of honor and carrying large cascading bouquets of gardenias and stephanotis, were Terry Hummel Slattery, sister-in-law of the bride, Rita Randolph Hunter, Carol M. Leslie and Linda Dean Huggins. Nieces of the bride and groom served as junior bridesmaids and also wore matching sapphire blue gowns, similar headpieces and floral arrangements. They were Shayla Suzanne Hewitt, Shannon Sullivan Hewitt, Kathleen Sullivan Reilly and Michelle Therese Slattery.

Kevin M. Slattery, nephew of the bride, dressed in a black tuxedo, served as ring bearer and carried a lace trimmed pillow cross-stitched by Terry Hummel Slattery.

Gift bearers for the ceremony were Mary Ann Reilly Hewitt, sister of the groom, and Charla Larkin Reilly, sister-in-law of the groom.

The groom wore a Spencer black tuxedo with pleated white wing collar shirt, satin bow tie and cummerbund. He wore an orchid and stephanotis as a boutonniere. Jerry H. Reilly was his brother's best man. Groomsmen were Dr. Jack L. Hewitt, brother-in-law of the groom, Representative Slattery, and J. R. Reilly and Michael C. Reilly, nephews of the groom. They each wore a tuxedo in black sharkskin with satin notched lapels, pleated white wing collar shirts with pearl studs, a black satin bow tie and cummerbund. Each groomsman and usher wore a single gardenia with stephanotis as their boutonniere.

Those seating guests as ushers were Terry L. Campbell, Rick Schneider, Larry Schneider, Dr. Terrace A. Bidnick, Michael "Bo" Conrad, Salvatore J. Marsalla, Frederick R. Wyrsch, Kenneth J. Reilly, Paudie O'Conner, Dr. Eamon C.J. McDwyer and William Leslie.

A traditional Catholic church service was held with "The Lord's Prayer" sung by Helen E. Yates. "Bless O Lord These Rings" was sung by Mary Kaye Pape and David Miller as Father Jerry spoke the words in blessing the wedding rings. After the exchange of vows and rings, David A. Miller sang "Like A Seal On Your Heart." During the sharing of the Eucharist, Tom L. Sack sang "Here I Am Lord."

The couple placed an arrangement of silk magnolia blossoms before the Blessed Mother's altar as a solo of "Ave Maria" was sung by Mary Kaye Pape. A special wedding blessing by Father Jerry was followed by an Irish Blessing read by Dr. McDwyer. The junior bridesmaids and other attendants exited to "Trumpet Voluntary," pausing in the aisle. A transition was then made of the music into "Reach Out and Touch," sung by Roxie Whitaker and Helen E. Yates with all others joining. The bridal party passed out white carnations with the newlywed couple greeting their guests while walking down the aisle.

A string ensemble consisting of Margaret Davis Kew, Patricia Carr, Jamie Kew and Ana Tello provided music at the church and a special song entitled "Right from the Heart" was sung prior to the ceremony by the groom.

Special floral arrangements included two bouquets in honor of the deceased parents which included a grouping of sheet music to represent the late Marian C. Reilly, a well-known singer; a violin to represent the late Edward F. Reilly Sr., a favorite instrument of the former mayor of Leavenworth; and sheaves of wheat in memory of the late Charles B. Slattery, a noted Atchison farmer. Each arrangement included white roses and freesia. The doors to the church were decorated with springeri and large white bows as well as the choir loft which also contained stephanotis. Yellow mums were grouped together and lined the steps in front of the church. Attached to alternating pews were brass candle holders adorned with white carnations, springeri, variegated and green pittostorum, strands of pearls, and Queen Anne's lace.

The wedding coordinator was Bernice L. Lessig. Sound coordinators were Ron Cowan and Sister Julia. Kitty O'Reagan served as liturgy coordinator and the wedding programs were distributed by Marilyn Domann Buehler and Chris Pollard Heider.

A reception was held at the Fort Leavenworth Officer's Club with entertainment provided for the over 2,000 guests by Lou and Carla Marek's band, "The Rainbow Express," by Alan Malaby and Lester D. Dalton as organists, and the Margaret Davis Kew string ensemble.

The gifts were attended by Sharon Efrid, Angela S. Wiley, and Alice Schneider.

Following a honeymoon, the couple will be at home at Leavenworth.

After that lengthy courtship and fairytale wedding, we enjoyed fifteen years of wedded bliss, but our happiness did not continue.

Luci's death in 2000 was a tragedy for me. I realized too late that I shouldn't have waited so many years to marry her, because she was my wife for only fifteen years. I should have proposed ten years earlier. But those fifteen years were terrific, and we had the blessing of Joseph to top it off. I still remember him in bed between us for the six months we both had the privilege of caring for him.

I remember so well the funeral service when Joe's nanny Cindee wheeled him into the church his mother loved and was such a part of. The Archbishop James P. Keleher conducted Luci's service.

The governor and the entire state Senate, both parties, attended that service, a surprise to me and most everyone else. I shall never forget arriving that morning at the church and wondering why so many law enforcement vehicles were present. Apparently escorting the Senate and Kansas governor was anticipated by our local law enforcement, but not by me. To say the least, it was a real tribute to Luci and her brother Jim and family.

Since Luci chose to be buried in Leavenworth, soon after her passing we decided to have a memorial service at St. Matthew's Cathedral in Washington, DC, the site of John F. Kennedy's funeral. Our dear friend and current pastor, Father Sam Giese, celebrated the mass. The number attending surprised us all, and the priest finally had to say "Ed and Jim, we have to begin the service as we have other masses." Her brother and I were busy greeting the attendees, thanking them for coming to the beautiful memorial service in her honor. To express our gratitude, we hosted a reception at the University Club.

Joe Pacholski, who began his job as a parole examiner with the US Parole Commission the year Luci died, observed my actions on the Commission that year and the rest of my tenure with the agency. In a July 2023 interview, Pacholski shared some observations. He said the most important thing he noticed was "how the chairman was able to remain focused on doing the right thing for everyone else, because technically, his world was crumbling.

"That is the secret of his management style," Pacholski said. "He was obviously rattled, going from party boy to married to a dad, then having it ripped apart," but I was focused on the fact that I was responsible for other's lives and for my own. Pacholski added, "I think it shows an enormous amount of character in an individual. He managed work, he managed that, and he managed his own loss."

One way I coped with the loss was by attending a men's group conducted by the National Presbyterian Church. Cindee Jacobs, who has helped me raise Joseph for years, suggested the group that focused on dealing with grief. Bob and Elizabeth Dole attended that church in Washington, DC, and I had attended a few services. Attending that group for months helped me, and I plan to talk to my own Catholic Church about a similar offering.

8

Having Children

My decision to marry was a shock to most who knew me. But Luci and I finally decided it was time to quit fooling around and either settle down or split—of course, her father had a lot to do with me making up my mind that evening in the cupboard. From the moment we tied the marriage knot, it was our intention to have children; I believe my wife, coming from a family of three, had that number in her head. For me it was just a matter of wondering whether this old guy in his late fifties could produce enough vital semen to permeate my wife's egg or eggs. I was obviously an optimist.

I have vivid memories of going to the fertility doctor to check on my viability after Lucy had a miscarriage sometime in the two years before Joseph's birth. That experience was an eye-opener to the trauma many couples go through being tested and waiting for results. When I arrived at the doctor's office, I saw several young men obviously nervous and embarrassed about why they were there. Since I was a senior citizen, I had no problem when the nurse called my name.

We pursued the challenge most couples endure, either in having children or failing to do so. We prayed, at least I did, to Saint Joseph. I'm certain Luci, with her strong faith, was showering the heavens with her prayers. Both of us earnestly prayed for a healthy child, be it a girl or a boy. What we went through is an even stronger indication of the love we had for one another, trying for children at our ages. Luci was sure she previously had a miscarriage, and the doctors said this often occurred with cystic fibrosis patients. So the new experience began when the doctor asked me to undergo some tests. I certainly remember when the nurse took me to an exam room and requested a semen sample. I have vivid memories of that day and the setting.

The setting was sterile. The lovely black nurse directed me to the lazy boy recliner and informed me what she needed. At my age, and after seven years of marriage, I understood the mission. Next to the lazy boy was a magazine rack with some quite exotic magazines. The nurse informed me if I needed help, I should refer to the magazine rack. If that didn't work, I was directed to click on the TV, which was programmed for an even more erotic performance. I could take as long as I liked, she quickly pointed out. When I left, I wasn't to come back through the reception area—rather I was to go out a door to the hall. Before leaving, I was to put the sample in a cabinet and press the button on the wall for the lab tech to pick it up. All this was necessary because the doctor was concerned about the viability of my semen. I understood they promptly test with hamster eggs to determine whether you could even have a child. After finishing the mission, all I could think of was all those other nervous young guys who were about to undergo the test. They hadn't yet met the great nurse who would introduce them to what was expected, but I'm sure most knew what they had to do. So here we are today with the blessing of our one and only: born on August 26, 1999, another Edward F. Reilly with the middle name Joseph. That was to honor the saint who heard our prayers.

Our decision to have a child at our ages obviously causes questions about the wisdom of doing so. But from day one of our marriage, we decided we had an obligation. The love we had for one another and the desire to pass it on were critical factors in that decision. If Luci had lived, there is no doubt in my mind that she would have wanted more children. Her loss was tragic for all of us and raised another question with many friends who wondered how this baby could be raised, since I was engaged full-time at the Justice Department as chairman of the US Parole Commission. I remember wondering too when Luci was in the hospital and Joseph was somewhere between two and three months old. One week I had no one to care for Joseph, so I had to take him to work with me. My office staff members handled it well, and probably even enjoyed the couple of days he accompanied me. They discovered he fit perfectly in the bottom drawer of one of their file cabinets, so that became his impromptu bed.

When word got around about the situation, God once again came to the rescue. An elderly grandmother in western Kansas who knew one of our Slattery clan said she would be happy to go to Washington and lend assistance for a while. So into our lives stepped Millie Vinduska, who had been working in the school cafeteria. She called and said, "Mr. Reilly, if you will pay my way, I will come back and help you out for as long as I'm able." As I recall, Millie had about five or six grandchildren. I couldn't believe what I was hearing but gladly accepted her offer since Luci was in hospital, and the outlook wasn't promising that she would recover from a CF infection. At about the same time, my brother-in-law Jim and I were at the hospital to visit Luci when I received a call from Ireland from Mae Gannon, the wife of General Michael Gannon. A graduate of the Command and General Staff College at Fort Leavenworth, General Gannon was the Honor Graduate, the top international officer, that year.

I nearly dropped the phone when I answered and Mae said, "We know you are in trouble with the baby and your wife in the hospital. I will be happy to come and take Joe and raise him here in Ireland with my children." As I recall, she had four children of her own. I did drop the phone at that point. But when I regained my composure, I knew there was no way my wife would ever forgive me if I didn't accept the responsibility for bringing this child into our lives. But I can only marvel at this Irish family's love and concern for the plight of others to offer to be his parents. Much later, during my visit with Joe to Belfast as International Observer to the Peace Fund, we traveled with Mike and Mae to the North, and I told Joe the story as we drove the road from Kildare to the North. As you might imagine, it was a moving time, and we all shed some tears. At least I did, and I believe Joe was somewhat shocked. Our trip to the North was eventful, as we were able to walk the Peace Bridge with the General and Mae. It gave us time to reflect on the Leavenworth years when Luci and I sponsored the Gannons and became a part of their family, as we did all the other Irish officers we sponsored during my time in Kansas before the Washington position. The rest of the story is filled with the lives of others who stepped up to counsel and support Joe, from neighbor Elinor Zemin giving him his first bottle, to a lady he referred to as Grandma Selma Forager whose husband owned some area hardware stores. They supplied Joe with almost all of his toys, including his first red wagon, tricycle, and bicycle. The condo Joe called home had a great influence on his life, as all the neighbors have taken an interest in his welfare. But the truth is, Joe has had so many ladies who have been a part of both our lives. One, who recalls being considered his foster mom, was Cindee Jacobs from the Philippines, who was with us for more than fifteen years. Lite Labette, also of the Philippines, helped her. Cindee took on the task from Millie Vinduska, who had to return to her grandchildren in western Kansas. But this was after the two of them dressed him in his baptismal gown for Father Bill Haegelin to baptize him at Georgetown hospital, where Luci was hospitalized for more than five months. Fortunately, even though she was on oxygen, the nurses brought Luci down for the service with the family. The entire ceremony was filmed by my former chief of staff and great friends, Peter and Roberta Hoffman. Would you believe they had even provided the baptismal bowl for the chapel, which did not have a fountain at that time? That bowl is now part of Joe's most touching memorabilia since the Hoffmans recently gave it to us.

Then Aunt Linda Slattery stepped in and stayed with him at Children's Hospital when he experienced his first minor operations. Also caring for Joe were Blanc Arias of Columbia; Bessie Georgia; and his honorary Aunt Katie Wyrsch. Also part of our Reilly family were Margarita and Hector Gavial. Margarita and Hector were with us in Kansas for more than thirty-five years, and they played a great role in maintaining the Reilly firm and our residence for all those years.

9

Close It Down

I endured quite a convoluted experience coming to Washington, DC, from a city of thirty-five thousand with the mission of closing the United States Parole Commission. This was a big assignment for someone whose only experience in the field of corrections had been to grow up in the shadows of the oldest and most famous federal prison in the nation, known in its early days as "The Big House." The home I was raised in was just twenty blocks from the reservation on Metropolitan Avenue. That's also the home of Fort Leavenworth, where you can find the United States Disciplinary Barracks, which houses most military prisoners of all branches of the service.

Senator Dole informed me of my confirmation when Luci and I were walking in a parade at the Leavenworth County Fair in Tonganoxie. Sheriff Terry Campbell advised me I had to take the senator's call. After finding out what we were doing, Senator Dole, one of my most stalwart supporters, had one question: "I thought you said you were leaving the Legislature, so why are you in a parade campaigning?"

I quickly explained that I wasn't running; rather, I was with the Reilly Company float trying to sell real estate. "Well, we're voting for your confirmation right now, so find a judge and do it quickly before someone changes their mind," the senator declared.

Judge Arthur J. Stanley was the man. I called him at home and told him I needed to be sworn in. He said, "Be at the federal building in the morning at 11 a.m. and we will do it." The event was in the federal magistrate's courtroom in the upstairs of Leavenworth's US Post Office.

Judge Stanley, another stalwart of America as well as a federal judge, was delighted to learn of the appointment. As I recall, the Federal Bureau of Investigation visited him, since I'd named him as a reference. I'm confident he gave me a thumbs up, or we wouldn't have been going the next morning to take the oath.

The judge was one of the most impressive jurists I ever met; he was known for his sense of humor and stately presence. After all, he stood nearly seven feet tall. I remember walking with him in one of the Veterans Day parades, and I realized even then what an honor that was.

It was clear in my interviews with the White House and Justice Department that my appointment was for five years, 1992–1997. During that period, the United States Parole Commission's offices in Dallas and Kansas City were to be shuttered. Its headquarters in Chevy Chase, Maryland, was to have its doors closed at the end of 1997. The prevailing sentiment during the years immediately before my appointment was that parole was too often "soft on crime" and permitted dangerous, antisocial individuals to reenter society and commit more criminal offenses—some very serious.

I began my assignment at the Commission after completing twenty-nine years in the Kanas Legislature, and I was earnest in my desire to fulfill the mission. Luci and I arrived in the Washington area in August 1992 and made our residence in Bethesda, Maryland, a lovely suburb of Washington that was within a few miles of the Commission headquarters in Chevy Chase. I was introduced to a group of devoted civil servants who took their jobs seriously and were deeply aware of the responsibility we all shared, ensuring that prisoners who were either released or reincarcerated were not a threat to public safety. Regardless of other priorities, the primary mission—ensuring the safety of the public—was unquestionably the most important.

Although I hadn't had employment or specific education in criminal justice, I had been a legislator who dealt with issues affecting the

Kansas prisons, including reforms in the prison system that resulted in higher salaries and better working conditions for prison personnel. I handled recruitment matters and participated in the establishment of vocational treatment programs and mental health counseling for prisoners. What I understood of the vernacular and practices employed by criminal justice professionals was learned through on-the-job training as a legislator.

I knew it was going to be difficult to transition into an appointed office, and from what I'd observed, I knew an appointee has to grow into the job. I needed to win staff over so they'd work with me, not against me. That was necessary to ensure that staff carried out the plans I set in motion. I knew the key was to get the careerists to buy into my goals.

At the beginning, all the staff, including the other commissioners, were suspicious of me. I was a politician, and they didn't know what to expect. I was also from the Midwest, and I was facing a lot of East Coasters. Myths abound about government bureaucrats or civil service employees—careerists—versus those the president appoints to office, who are usually confirmed by the Senate. In my opinion, the best way to achieve success is to eliminate these myths quickly.

Luckily, I got a copy of a Georgetown study that provided advice on transitioning into an appointed office, and it became my "Bible." I gave copies of it to top staff as well. This study detailed the university and IBM working together to identify how to engage when you're entering the federal system. The study emphasized forming a partnership to accomplish your mission. The only way I found successful was bringing the staff I'd inherited into my corner by setting a good example. Communication is paramount, which means seeking guidance from those already serving the government. If you don't, there will be a sad and humiliating end to your service.

Careerists have been a part of American history since 1883, when the Pendleton Act established the federal civil service system. This led to tension between career civil servants and appointees. Many thought adopting that system led to the placement of people because of partisan politics. As Andrew Jackson said in 1829, "No man has any more intrinsic right to official station than another."

History shows that the spoils system approach to staffing the government couldn't be sustained since elected politicians were swamped by job seekers. A government undergoing growth pains needs a more competent and dedicated group of public servants, whether careerists or appointees. Today, with the exception of a few thousand political appointees, most posts are held by full-time career employees who provide the services created by various administrations and Congress. How the one coming to Washington assimilates with these employees determines the success or failure of the appointee and the administration served.

We've all witnessed from administration to administration how critical it is to have a qualified group of potential staff. I remember a recent candidate for president said to those gathered at the election watch after the results were in, "Oh my God, I've been elected president!" In some ways I felt the same hysteria on the night of my elections, but I was confident I had folks ready to support and serve. They believed in what I was advocating for and were willing to commit themselves to ensuring our efforts were successful.

A study by the General Accounting Office concluded that the average tenure for a presidential appointee is just under three years. They're often referred to as "in and outers" because they don't last that long if they've failed in recognizing not only the rules of engagement but also that they have many bosses. Our system of government allows the president to reward his or her loyalists with an appropriate assignment. More importantly, the leadership he appoints has power over the government. The ability for the leader, in the case of the president, to assemble a staff in just eleven weeks after the November election, is a challenge. That's why you must have assembled a committed and competent team. That's all the more reason to avail yourself of the results of the Georgetown University study.

I quickly realized that political appointees face a lot of questions. Are you qualified for a particular job? After all, resumes often don't match the job to which you're appointed. And just how was the selection and confirmation achieved?

I felt fairly confident about my experience in the Kansas Legislature. I learned from one of the best, Dr. Karl Menninger; I had chaired a number of influential committees; I became aware and educated about the Kansas criminal justice system. So I felt my background was solid.

After becoming acquainted with what turned out to be a dedicated and loyal staff, I headed downtown to the headquarters of the United States Sentencing Commission to be briefed and meet the chairman. Congress created the Sentencing Commission in 1984 to assume responsibility for creating a sort of "Bible," which would dictate the penalties and sentences for federal crimes committed after 1987. The initiative was the result of public reaction to shocking stories of crimes committed by some parolees when they were released.

In its usual fashion, Congress reacted by abolishing an agency before really dissecting the internal problems of the parole process. I was aware that the chairman of the US Parole Commission was also an ex officio member of the Sentencing Commission, permitted to sit on the decision-making panel and provide at least limited counsel as the new commission established its agency and policies. William Walter Wilkins, a dear friend of South Carolina Senator Strom Thurmond, was the first chairman of the Sentencing Commission. Judge Wilkins was a former US appellate judge for the Fourth Circuit and also a former US district judge for the District of South Carolina.

The Charleston, South Carolina native served as chair from 1985 to 1994. His major responsibility was setting up the newly-established Sentencing Commission to replace the Parole Commission by 1997. The Parole Commission had been abolished by congressional action that also established a new sentencing structure. The Sentencing Commission was established in 1984, so when I arrived in 1992, it was in its development stages of crafting sentencing guidelines to assist the courts and judges in assessing penalties for offenses. Since this commission was to replace federal parole, it was designed to incorporate the purposes of sentencing—

just punishment, at least as seen at that time, deterrence, incapacitation, and rehabilitation.

The commission was to provide certainty and fairness by avoiding disparity among offenders with similar criminal conduct, while permitting judicial flexibility by taking aggravating and mitigating factors into account. This was Congress's response, going back to the Reagan years, to stem the violence flourishing because of drugs, especially crack cocaine.

In truth, the Sentencing Commission was a reincarnation of the US Parole Commission, which basically had the same charge. It was staffed with seven commissioners, practitioners in parole and criminal justice. They were more than capable of considering the elements of the crime and previous criminal conduct. Ironically, authors tweaked the parole guidelines to fashion the US sentencing guidelines. If you compare the two in their application, it becomes evident that the success of the Parole Commission played a big role in crafting the new policy.

Apparently, for that reason, Congress decided the attorney general and the chairman of the US Parole Commission should serve as ex officio commissioners. Our role was to offer counsel since we had no vote. I attended the National Institute of Justice school on parole in Boulder, so I was comfortable with parole guidelines, and the sentencing guidelines were similar. In my opinion, Congress seemed driven to create another body to answer the frustration about increasing violent crime. What they crafted didn't change much of what the Parole Commission was doing successfully before I arrived on the scene. But judges now had the criminal "Bible" that dictated sentences, creating a degree of unrest within the judiciary. But it gave others the option of saying the sentence was mandatory and not subject to parole.

As it turned out, the folks who contacted me about their experience of getting caught up in an offense with a set sentence were shocked. It was definitely a wake-up call for many citizens who ended up in court. Even a prominent congressman who pushed for the enabling legislation was shocked when we told him the Parole Commission could do nothing to help a friend of his, since his was a determinate sentence.

It was an easy out for the judges, even though they had some flexibility to depart from a guideline within certain ranges. A federal judge who helped craft the guidelines, Marvin Frankel, said judges weren't invoking their departure authority even when doing so would create more appropriate sentences. The new system of sentencing didn't always take into consideration extraordinary circumstances the federal Parole Commission could consider. Rather, a section of the guidelines declared that a defendant's family ties and responsibilities are not ordinarily relevant in departure analysis. I would argue that when we tinker with what is already working, we can anticipate a different set of problems.

Unlike the Parole Commission, the Sentencing Commission is an independent agency within the judicial branch, and it is composed of members appointed by the president and confirmed by the Senate for six-year terms. Working together, we carried out our mandate, even trying to amend what we found were disparate sentences, such as crack versus cocaine sentencing—to no avail, since Congress rejected our proposals several times.

Only in the nation's capital could you be given the mission of closing a parole agency while Congress was in the process of passing legislation that impacted the law abolishing parole for federal offenders. Taking over District of Columbia parole cases in 1997–1998 and finally closing the local Lorton prison in 2001 cast a new light on the US Parole Commission. It meant we inherited some nine thousand local offenders, many of whom were parole eligible. It placed the Commission in the position of shifting gears from closing the agency to bringing on staff who had been displaced to handle the new case load.

Jasper Clay, who served on the Commission with me for four years, said in an April 2023 interview he was no longer serving on the Commission when Lorton closed, but he worked for the Commission on contract for an additional year because the workload increased. His work involved transitioning to the 1997–1998 DC initiatives.

Commissioner Cranston Mitchell, nominated by President Bush in 2003, said in an April 2023 interview that the tools developed for use with the federal offenders didn't apply well to the DC criminals. "They came from a different community and were a different kind of offender," Mitchell said. "We had to come up with different modalities, as the federal offenders were sophisticated criminals, and the DC prisoners were more urban."

In a June 2023 interview, Thomas Hutchison, appointed chief of staff for the Commission after Peter Hoffman retired, described the DC crimes as more state and local, like murder and assault and battery. Joe Pacholski, who became a parole examiner for the Commission in 2000, said in a July 2023 interview that "Ed decided to fight for the DC cases and got them," and I confirmed that had been the case. "For an individual who was supposed to be closing down an agency, he saw the value of what its core function was," Pacholski noted. "Too many functions were being utilized [that closing it down] wasn't a good idea."

Hutchinson said working with Lorton was difficult. "Early on we were told to go down to a ceremony there on the closing," he cited as an example. "We got there, and it had been cancelled."

The process "caused a lot of problems," Hutchinson said. Not only were there "special rules for the DC cases, we also had trouble finding places for the hearings in and around DC. The large numbers were also a problem."

Hutchinson also recalls:

> The Commission was highly criticized when it took over the DC cases because we were considered outsiders coming in. But the fact is, Reilly was good at this. We were just as much a part of the community as anyone. The public discussions in DC included people who represented the parolees. We went out of our way to act as good citizens of the community, and Ed deserves the credit for that.
>
> We did outreach into the community as much as we could. Ed was very good at that, and also he was very conscientious. We were trying to coordinate activities with various part of the government to include the judiciary and the police, and we behaved as if we were citizens of DC.

I especially remember one social event in DC during the Lorton days. As chairman of the commission and a former Jaycee, I was extended an invitation to a dinner featuring a special secret guest. We were seated awaiting the arrival of the honored guest, who was to be seated next to me. Who should it be but former DC Mayor Marion Barry?

Barry was famous, or perhaps infamous, for a number of scandals and crimes during his lengthy stay in office as mayor and council member. The Federal Bureau of Investigation raided one of his hangouts in 1990 and caught him smoking crack cocaine and cavorting with a prostitute. The story is that they didn't want to notify local officials for fear the mayor would be alerted. He served six months for that.

I must give credit where credit is due: Mayor Barry was a consummate politician. By the time he met and visited with me about my role, you would have thought we had known each other for years. When he was called on to speak, it was all about our friendship and service. He was purportedly delighted that I was his guest, especially since I was chairman of the US Parole Commission and the Department of Corrections, under which he had served time for his misdeeds. In spite of all his scandals and alleged crimes, which included tax evasion and bribery, the mayor was extremely popular in Washington, DC. He handed out turkeys over the holidays, and many of the hungry were fed by the Barry campaign.

When Lorton closed, I predicted public outcry in the District about displacing incarcerated loved ones from the local area and sending them to federal institutions across the country. I thought it might bring back the violence of the 1960s. Frankly, I never thought the bill would pass, but a lot of political pressure brought about the land grab for the Lorton land, which overlooked Occoquan, a historic town in Prince William County, Virginia.

The pros and cons of the congressional action were a lesson, since the District of Columbia was anxious to get rid of the financial burden of running Lorton. Real estate developers wanted the land, and Congress was displeased with the lax operation of the Virginia institution, partly because some inmates were coming and going on weekend furloughs.

There were some protests in the community, nonviolent but forceful. Nevertheless, Congress managed to slip through the change very quickly, something we don't often witness.

As a result, the Federal Bureau of Prisons now incarcerates all District of Columbia and federal offenders, to include the remaining parole-eligible offenders. The Bureau also housed new law-violators who were to fall under either the Administrative Office of the Courts or Court Services Offender Supervision Agency for the District of Columbia. At the time, the District of Columbia offenders in federal prisons were supposed to be within five hundred miles of the District of Columbia so their families could visit them.

Sam Brownback, US senator from Kansas from 1996 to 2011, was instrumental in getting this guideline established, as he amended the bill concerning the Lorton prison to provide that inmates be within five hundred miles of DC. This was quite a change from when they were all within the limits of Washington, DC. The controversy revolved around the distance spouses and children must travel to visit their loved ones. According to the current BOP designation guidelines, an attempt is still made to adhere to the five-hundred-mile limit.

Michael Gaines, President Clinton's appointee to the Commission, had just been designated chairman in 1997, when the agency was to take over the DC responsibilities. Clinton appointed him to the Commission in 1995, but I continued serving as chairman during his first term. Mike served as chairman in his second term.

In an August 2023 interview, Gaines said the transition with DC "went better than I thought it probably would." There had been a lot of discussion before the law was enacted, he noted. "And it pretty much fell into place," he said. "Once it was the law, it was the law, and this is how you're going to do it."

He reiterated how much different the DC inmates' crimes were than the federal crimes the Commission was more familiar with, prompting some changes in the Commission's guidelines. "They were very much like the crimes I saw as chairman of the Arkansas parole board," a position he held from 1989 to 1994. They included burglaries and assaults, among other crimes. "Generally speaking, those doing federal time have committed very sophisticated, white-collar crimes," Gaines noted.

There was a concern "that our offices were in Chevy Chase. That's right across the line from DC, but we weren't in DC. There was some controversy that if we were doing DC, we should be in DC," Gaines recalled. During his tenure as chairman, he and other staff "spent time with the General Services Administration," which handles federal real estate, "and after I left, the offices moved into the District." They remain there today at 90 K Street NE, Washington DC.

10

Being Chairman

The president designates who is to serve as chairman of the United States Parole Commission and the term they are to serve. The attorney general names the vice chairman of the agency along with the term they serve. Being named chairman was not a major surprise considering my background as former chair of major committees in the Kansas Legislature. Nevertheless, it is frightening to realize you are now working not with governors but with presidents of the United States.

I learned long ago that assuming leadership is one of life's most difficult assignments. You have to make decisions that aren't always pleasant. It would be easier to ignore these issues, but to lead also means being responsive to a higher authority; this should never be taken lightly, as we are all accountable to someone. I recognized early that if you're going to work for someone, you must serve them with integrity, gratitude, and the determination to finish well no matter what position you hold. As chairman, I realized that with leadership comes accountability for our actions, conduct, and carrying out the mission assigned. Being chairman of the United States Parole Commission was a great honor, and in my opinion, equated to another degree in criminal justice.

I've given quite a bit of thought to what it takes to make it as chairman or a new parole board member. It means accepting the reality that you have a position and responsibility that impacts many individuals and families. Of course, there are the offenders and victims, both of whom are significantly affected. But you also need to consider the community, the taxpayers, keeping in mind the cost of incarcerating a person for years. You must realize the United States incarcerates more people than any other country, outranking Russia and China.

But besides this, after you've been on the job for a while, you may have earned a reputation as a pushover liberal or a hard ass. There must be humility coupled with wisdom, knowledge and compassion for those in our charge. If anyone told you it was a meaningless political job, they weren't dealing with reality. I found it one of the most challenging posts you could occupy, but I felt comfortable in the position after attending the training. That and legislative experience helped me fulfill the mission.

As noted, as chairman of the Parole Commission, I was also an ex officio member of the US Sentencing Commission. At one point, Sentencing Commission members were invited to visit some inmates at the US Penitentiary near Lewisburg, PA, and Luci was eager to go along. I was hesitant at first about her going into still another penitentiary—she already had been inside USP Leavenworth.

Since other staff were also going, she was permitted to accompany us, and along with a group of federal judges, we rode a bus to Pennsylvania. I remember previously visiting that facility during a parole hearing when inmates were protesting and throwing things out of the cell windows, so I wasn't sure what we'd see this time. This time our afternoon visit went well. Several inmates were brought to a conference room and seated in front. There were probably about twelve present, along with prison staff. Inmates were invited to discuss their stories, and they'd also prepared questions. Their stories were almost all the same, except for a few expletives.

Most provided a brief description of their crime, the sentence handed down, and the unfairness of the court or judge's decision. Those of us working in the system heard this so often it was redundant. The story included a rotten parent—mother or father—or the relative with whom they'd lived. Almost every inmate blamed someone else for the situation they were in. When all their stories had been hashed out, the warden asked if anyone had questions. No one responded, but after the second request, my never-fearing wife said, "Yes, I have a question for each of you, and I want each of you to answer the same question."

I was in shock, as I wasn't sure what was going to come out of her mouth. Then in true Luci educator style, she asked, "Well, you have blamed everyone in your lives, but what about yourselves? When do you accept and blame yourself for what you've done?" There was a lot of stammering and stuttering as they tried to take another approach or started ad-libbing. None of us was quite sure what would come next, but the judges were anxious to get back on the bus and head back to Washington. Once on the bus, they told Luci how impressed they were that she asked the question, since they knew they'd often been blamed for the sentences.

When I began my service with the criminal justice system, I had no idea I would be involved in so many aspects of the field. As a reserve Leavenworth County deputy for years under various sheriffs, I usually had a firearm within easy reach. The Parole Commission reviewed a lot of big cases, including drug offenders, Mafiosi, spies, drug cartel killers, and terrorists, to name a few. So I was obviously exposed to many dangerous possibilities, such as being kidnapped by a drug cartel. While I was chairman, I participated in what was known as a Transfer Treaty exchange. That meant the United States returned Mexican offenders who had been in United States prisons in exchange for a number of American prisoners in Mexican prisons. These inmates, I'm sure, couldn't wait to get back on United States soil to be debriefed by the Bureau of Prisons. They were eager to tell what they'd endured while incarcerated in the federal prison in Juarez.

As the Parole Commission chairman, I represented the United States and signed the treaty exchange just as the deputy attorney general of Mexico did for Mexico. I vividly remember crossing the border in a United States Bureau of Prisons carryall and being met by a cadre of Mexican federal police cars and motorcycles carrying men armed with machine guns on their shoulders. It was an impressive but frightening scene. As we raced at sixty miles an hour through Juarez, police waved madly for pedestrians and bicyclists to either move out of the way or be killed.

These and other experiences convinced me that serving on the Commission definitely had its share of danger. My conviction was reinforced a hundredfold in 1999 when Luci and I had a son. The United States Marshals Service appointed me as a special marshal, which gave me permission and commission to carry a firearm. I was required to qualify with a firearm under the watchful eye of a Marshals Service range officer. However, I hated to carry a weapon, as one pant leg was always longer than the other because of the weapon's weight.

You may wonder whether I carried the weapon on the many flights I was required to take as Parole Commissioner. I often did, but never when my son Joseph was there. I thought it would be too much of a challenge to explain why a special deputy marshal, who was also a senior citizen, was carrying a weapon and shepherding a ten-year-old boy.

*****

Some of you may have concluded that we folks from Kansas are "cowboys," or "buckeroos," as it was so well expressed in Paramount Pictures' 1990 hit, *The Hunt for Red October*. You would be partially correct, for in some parts of Kansas it's not uncommon to see a pickup truck displaying a rifle or shotgun in the back window. Since Kansas has an open carry law, you can carry a firearm if it's not concealed.

Leavenworth and the surrounding area has its own history of well-known cowboys, namely Buffalo Bill Cody. He was born in Iowa but came to Leavenworth with his family when he was about nine. When they arrived in June 1854, they built a seven-room log cabin in Salt Creek Valley, just north of Fort Leavenworth. Immediately after his arrival, his father Isaac secured an Army contract to supply hay to the fort.

Only thirteen weeks after his arrival, Isaac got into a heated argument with a pro-slavery neighbor, who knifed him. Isaac never fully recovered from this serious wound. He died from complications from the wound, leaving eleven-year-old Bill the man in the family. Because of his connection with roomers his mother took in, Bill got a job driving a team of oxen to town at fifty cents a day.

The next job for the twelve-year-old Bill was running messages for the Overland Freight Company of Russell, Majors and Waddell in Leavenworth. This proved too dull, and he became the herdsman for a large herd of oxen the company owned. But he got in a fight with a much larger boy and used a knife on him. To avoid arrest, he hid out in a wagon train, and the wagon master persuaded his mother to let him hire on as a drover for the trains' extra oxen. Thus began the first of many adventures. By the time he was fifteen, he was a Pony Express rider.

Before the Civil War ended, Bill enlisted and met his future wife, Louisa Frederici. He married her once he was out of the Army, though it was a contentious relationship throughout many years. He then signed on with the Kansas Pacific Railroad to provide meat for the construction crews. In the next eighteen months, he shot 4,280 buffalo, which is how he got the nickname of "Buffalo Bill." He later earned a reputation as a scout on several campaigns with the Frontier Army.

But this hard-riding, hard-drinking sharpshooter became a western folk history hero after an author known as Ned Buntline catapulted him to fame, first in newspaper articles and later in dime novels. By 1883, he started his Wild West Show, often playing before the crowned heads around the world. Handbills around the city of Leavenworth attest that Leavenworth citizens also had the opportunity to attend the show.

* * * * *

Though my time on the Commission often provided many adventures, the time came when I had to move on. When I retired from the Parole Commission, United States Marshals Service Director Chris Dudley and my close friend, Bob Finan, recognized my service as a special deputy and presented me with my badge and a certificate of recognition.

For the majority of my time on the Parole Commission, I served as chairman, since that was a presidential appointment. When President Bill Clinton was elected in 1992, he opted not to immediately select a new chairman. Rather, he appointed Michael Gaines as a commissioner in 1995. After Clinton was elected to a second term, he designated Gaines as chairman in 1997. Gaines had served Clinton in Arkansas as a member of his executive staff and Clinton wanted him to serve as chairman for a period of time. During that time, I served as chairman of the National Appeals Board. The significance of mentioning this is twofold. Most importantly, it was a peaceful transition, and I notified staff of the decision and the support we needed to extend to the new chairman. If we could see this kind of transition today in public life, how great the public's expectations would be.

"We actually had two transitions," Gaines noted in an August 2023 interview. "[Reilly] was chairman when I came on as commissioner, and he served in that role through Clinton's first term. Then the powers that be thought he needed to name his own chairman." He figures that was because the chairman is an ex officio member of the Sentencing Commission and also serves on a board that administers grants to states to help them deal with parole and probation issues.

Gaines considered it a good transition, too. "He was great. His personality works so well, because if there's ever been a people person, it's Ed Reilly."

Before his confirmation, Gaines recalls, "He had my wife [Kay] and me to dinner and we went to an Aretha Franklin concert with him and Luci."

The Commission got along "very well," Gaines said. "It was like family. We were this little group of commissioners, and we had to take care of each other. The staff was a lot bigger than us, and they knew more about things than we did. There was a lot of collegiality, especially among Ed, Jasper Clay, John Simpson, and me." Another commissioner was in Florida, and he came to the office only sporadically.

"I've learned to celebrate Saint Patrick's Day in a much bigger way knowing Ed Reilly," Gaines quipped. "I remember once Ed serenaded my wife and I with 'Danny Boy' when we were at a restaurant. And he often took some of us to an Irish pub."

Gaines called it a "good work environment." He'd been shocked because all the other commissioners had been appointed by a Republican president. "But we became like a family, and it wasn't difficult," he said. "I give a lot of that credit to Ed."

Though they might disagree on something occasionally, Gaines said they never reached a level that could be considered a spat. Marie Ragghianti was named Gaines's chief of staff. Marie was best known for being the whistleblower who exposed Tennessee Governor Ray Blanton's "clemency for cash" scandal in 1977–1979. She was chairman of the Tennessee parole board when she discovered this.

"I can't imagine being in that position and the political pressure she was under because Blanton had appointed her," Gaines said.

Her story was the subject of a 1983 book by Peter Maas: *Marie: A True Story* and in 1985 was made into a movie by the same name. Gaines said Fred Thompson, who was her attorney, played himself in the movie, and this started his acting career. President Clinton, in a recess appointment, named her to the US Parole Commission.

A president can make a recess appointment when Congress is out of session. The term is usually for a year or two and it requires no Senate confirmation, Gaines said. She served as his vice chairman. When George W. Bush was elected, Thompson got her an appointment to fill Gaines's seat, since he resigned, but the Senate failed to confirm her. When Gaines resigned, he started working for a government public relations firm run by James Lee Witt, the director of the Federal Emergency Management Agency in the Clinton administration.

Ed and Luci attending a function of the Order of the Holy Sepulcher at the Cathedral Basilica of St. Louis. (Photo courtesy of the author's collection)

Ed with longtime movie star Maureen O'Hara at the White House in 1984. Both were potential nominees for the post of ambassador to Ireland during the Reagan administration and remained friends over the years. (Photo courtesy of the author's collection)

Ed's grandfather, Humphrey Reilly, with other Leavenworth County employees at the county courthouse. A longtime county official, he had served as county treasurer. (Photo courtesy of the author's collection)

Ed's grandfather, Humphrey V. Reilly, served many terms as Leavenworth County treasurer. After losing his final campaign, he and Ed's father, Edward F. Reilly Sr., started a financial business in Leavenworth. (Photo courtesy of the author's collection)

Federal Magistrate Judge Arthur Stanley swears in Ed Reilly after he was confirmed as chairman of the US Parole Commission. The ceremony was in Stanley's office in Leavenworth. (Photo courtesy of the author's collection)

Leavenworth Ku Klux Klan members burned a cross in the lawn of Ed's grandfather before his last campaign for county treasurer, which he lost. The Leavenworth Klan was one of the last organized in Kansas in the 1920s, but it was strong. This photo shows a Ku Klux Klan funeral at a Baptist Church at Sixth and Seneca in Leavenworth. (Photo courtesy of the Kansas Historical Society)

This photo shows Kansas State Penitentiary in 1868, the first state prison, located in Lansing, Kansas. While in the Kansas Legislature, Ed was involved with many issues concerning the prison, including capital punishment. (Photo courtesy of the author's collection)

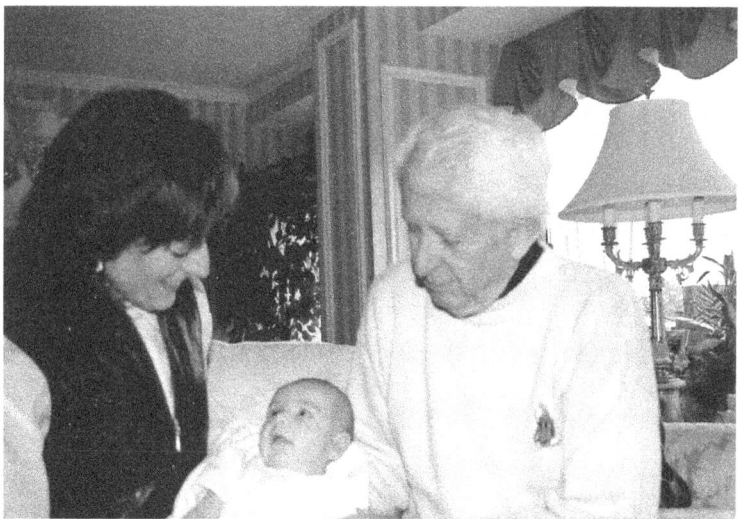

Luci and Ed look adoringly at their son, Joseph, when he was four months old. He was only six months old when Luci died. (Photo courtesy of the author's collection)

Ed's mother, Marian C. Sullivan Reilly, graduated with a music degree from St. Mary's College. Before meeting Ed's father, she had planned to pursue a career in music in New York City. (Photo courtesy of the author's collection)

Ed's father, Edward F. Reilly Jr., was elected Leavenworth mayor for several terms beginning in 1956. (Photo courtesy of the author's collection)

Ed was one of twenty-two escorts for Cardinal Francis George of Chicago at the sixtieth anniversary of the Normandy Invasion. The escorts were members of the Lumen Christi Institute of Chicago.

The Reilly and Slattery families celebrate another holiday in Leavenworth. Luci Slattery was married to Ed. This photo was taken in the great room at the Reillys' Leavenworth residence. (Photo courtesy of the author's collection)

Ed as a young Kansas legislator. He was elected in 1963 to fill a Leavenworth representative's unexpired term. (Photo courtesy of the author's collection)

The Reilly family in the mayor's office in Leavenworth City Hall. Mayor Reilly is seated at his desk surrounded by (from left) Ed, his sister Mary Ann, his mother Marian, and his brother Jerry. (Photo courtesy of the author's collection)

Ed's great-great grandfather, Captain Edward F. Reilly of Cavan, Ireland, fought in the Civil War battle of Wilson Creek in Springfield, Missouri. (Photo courtesy of the author's collection)

Members of the US Parole Commission during Ed's early days as commission chairman. Seated (from left) are Commissioners Vince Fechtel, Carol Getty, and Chief of Staff Henry Grinner. Standing, (from left), are Commissioners John Simpson, Jasper Clay, and Ed Reilly. (Photo courtesy of the author's collection)

→

The 1987 Kansas Senate is pictured in the Senate Chamber at the State Capitol in Topeka. Ed is at the far left in the third row. (Photo courtesy of the author's collection)

Ed (left) with Elizabeth and Bob Dole. Ed considers US Senator Bob Dole of Kansas his mentor and Dole was one of his strongest supporters in securing his appointment to the Parole Commission. (Photo courtesy of the author's collection)

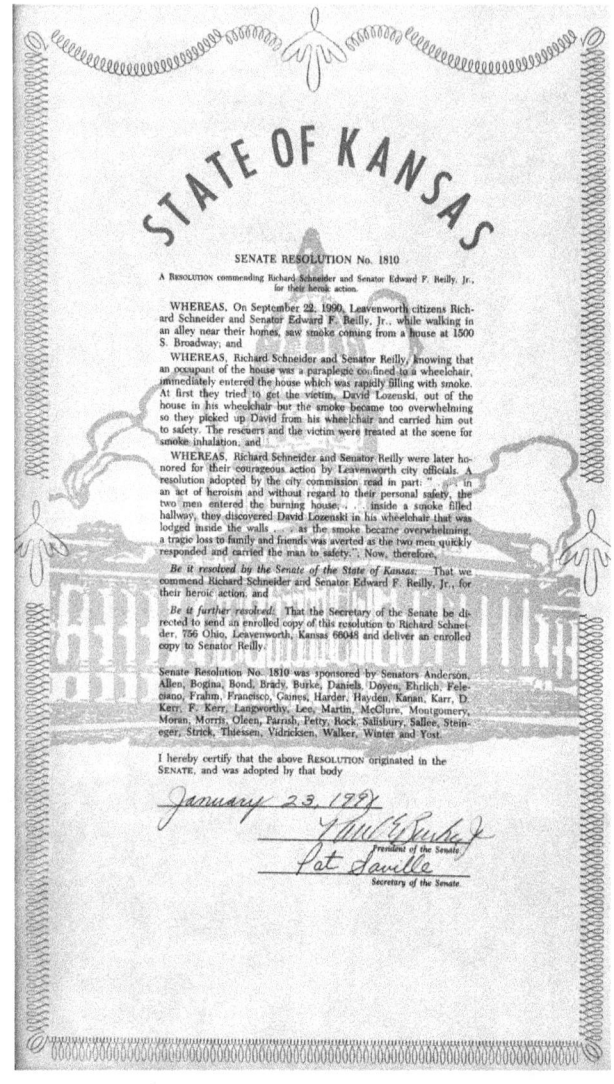

The Kansas Senate passed a resolution honoring the bravery of Ed and his neighbor, Rick Snyder, after they entered a burning house in Leavenworth and saved David Lozenski, whose mother was struggling to get him in his wheelchair out of the blazes. Reilly and Snyder were awarded the Carnegie Medal for Heroism for that act. (Photo courtesy of the author's collection)

Ed Reilly when he was about thirteen or fourteen months old. (Photo courtesy of the author's collection)

The KU basketball player known as "Wilt the Stilt" Chamberlain visited the Guardian Angel Orphanage in Leavenworth in 1959. Ed's father, pictured on the far right, presented Chamberlain with a key to the city. Ed and Wilt sat together in a geography class when both were students at the University of Kansas. (Photo courtesy of the author's collection)

11

Looking Back at the USPC

One day at the office, I received a phone call from Jasper Clay, former vice chairman of the United States Parole Commission. Jasper was one of my favorite commissioners when I came on board in October 1992 as the Commission chairman. We became great friends, and it wasn't until I was around for a year that I learned he and I had competed in the early eighties for a position on the Commission.

I had several interviews in Washington, DC, at that time while I was serving in the Kansas Senate. Monie Ryder interviewed me and then sent me to see United States Parole Commission Chairman Ben Baer. I never felt the interview with Chairman Baer went well. I thought he was really pushing for someone else from the Maryland area, and sure enough, Jasper Clay was the one who landed the position. It wasn't until ten years later when President George H. W. Bush designated me as chairman that Commissioner Clay walked in my office and asked, "Ed, have you ever seen this page from the Congressional Record?"

I was stunned when I read it, then looked up and asked, "How can you be speaking to me in view of this?" I learned from those records that my mentor, Bob Dole, was so upset I hadn't received the earlier appointment that he placed what is known as a legislative hold on Jasper Clay's nomination. In any event, we shook hands and felt like we had both succeeded, but to Jasper's credit, it took me ten years longer.

Clay, nominated by President Ronald Reagan to serve on the Commission in April 1984, recalled that hold in an interview in April 2023. He said Senator Dole finally decided to lift the hold because Clay had the support of all the Maryland legislators and two senators for the position. He was appointed vice chairman of the Commission.

"He was not aware of Dole's comments [which were in the Congressional Record]," Clay said. "I introduced him to the staff and told them he had persevered and fought for the position for ten years. I said they should be more like him."

When Clay made me aware of what had happened, "We became good friends as a result of this," Clay said. Clay said he made it a point to introduce me to "the outstanding staff members you should utilize," such as Peter Hoffman, "since he knows the total history. He wrote the history, and he did all the statistics and training, and he was an outstanding person." Peter Hoffman served as chief of staff from 1995 through 1997.

Clay said he wanted me to meet the outstanding staff members because he thought they could help me relate to the other employees. Clay served four years on the Commission while I was chairman.

"We will be friends for life," Clay said. "That's the kind of man Ed was. He made a significant increase in the Commission's credibility. He was an outstanding chairman, and I told Ed I had worked for 10 chairmen on the Maryland commission and the US Parole Commission."

I was delighted to be invited to the celebration of Jasper's ninetieth birthday on November 26, 2023. During the celebration, I had a chance to say publicly just how I feel about this man:

> What an honor and privilege to be here to celebrate the ninetieth birthday of a great colleague, personal friend, and a true American patriot. Serving both political parties is a tribute to the man who is loved by all that meet him. The opportunity I had to serve with him for some twenty years was a whole new degree for me in criminal justice, because he possesses so much knowledge in his fifty-plus years of giving back to those we were trying to restore and return to society.
>
> He believes, as I do, that most everyone has the ability to turn their

life if given that chance, be it first or second. Jasper is a human being that once he meets you, he will never forget you, because both lives were touched by his humor, love for another and for life. Well, my dear friend, you have proven your value for over ninety years to all of us. When I woke this morning, I flipped my daily prayer calendar and what did I find but the following, so appropriate as we salute you on ninety years.

The words of the Rev. Martin Luther King Jr.: "Everybody can be great, because everybody can serve. You don't need a college degree to serve. You don't have to make your subject and verb agree to serve. You only need a heart full of grace, a soul generated by love."

That is the man we celebrate today—God bless you, my friend, and many more years.

When I walked in as the chairman, I replaced Carol Pavilack Getty. I had previously met her though our respective careers, and we had had a professional social relationship. When I met her, I was a Kansas senator, and she headed the Arizona Parole Board. I had met with her several times before she was appointed to chair the USPC when Ben Baer died. Talk about strange events dealing in the political arena. You never want to piss anyone off, as you never know when you'll meet again, and under what circumstances. I was fortunate to have as my chief of staff at the time Henry Grinner, a man who was loyal, dedicated, and a real team player who could mend most any fence and conquer most opponents with his kindness and professionalism. Former Chief of Staff Peter Hoffman recently told me an anecdote related to Ms. Pavilack. She told him, when she learned I was seeking the chairmanship, "I thought he was after my body and instead he was after my job." When I came on as chairman, she remained on the Commission for several years. We remain friends today, and she lives across the river from Leavenworth in Missouri.

Chief of Staff Henry Grinner was able to build a coalition of loyal staff committed to accomplishing the mission of the Commission as well as fulfilling its responsibilities as an agency with public safety as its main goal. I learned early that to accomplish our mission, we needed staff who could work well together while respecting the philosophies that each of us brought to the table. Henry was a great helmsman at the Commission, and his loyalty was never in question; he just wanted to get the job done and done well.

Another man who served as chief of staff later in my tenure, Tom Hutchinson, indicated one reason he thought staff responded well. "I thought [Reilly] was very much a guy who was concerned about his staff, whether it was a secretary, file clerk, hearing examiner, or whoever. He was very careful to look out to see if things were good for them. He did things that other agencies weren't doing, like observing Black History Month, outings, picnics every summer."

At that time, the Commission was composed of six commissioners, with two regional offices and a central office in Chevy Chase, Maryland. The Dallas and Kansas City offices were staffed by some competent, long-serving associates who were well aware that I had been brought in to see that the Commission would be phased out and shut down by 1997.

Coming in, I had to inform career employees that I'd been brought in to do that. Certainly, I could have been viewed as the villain, but I worked to persuade everybody to get on board. The chief of staff was already on board. One way I did it was not just casting people out but helping them find jobs.

Parole had been abolished by the passage of the US Sentencing Reform Act in 1984 and had been surviving on extensions granted by Congress until 1997. I was charged with moving forward on the agency closure. In meetings with the attorney general and members of Congress, it was clear that the passage of the US Sentencing Reform Act, which abolished parole and established US sentencing guidelines, was the Holy Grail for the future sentencing policy in the United States.

It was apparent to me, but not my pleasure, that I had to move forward on closing the Dallas office first and later the Kansas City office. The closures meant the displacement of all the staff without them having bumping rights to relocate in the agency; in other words, they were terminated, and the offices were shut down. All the work of the regions moved to the central office in Chevy Chase, where we were trying to reduce staff and cut expenditures based on a congressional mandate. We did manage to absorb the work, and thanks to Chief of Staff Grinner and a committed group of commissioners and staff, we were able to complete our work while reducing the budget. Congress helped along through their cuts, but it was still a difficult time for me.

In closing down the offices, we had to get rid of sixty-some career employees. But I set out not to just fire them but to work to get them into some other federal agency. My staff said I was crazy, but I was determined. I felt an obligation to these employees. To accomplish it, I brought in people from the Justice Department of Personnel and made sure the displaced staff had the proper forms they needed. Most had been on board for at least three years, so they didn't have to reapply. Everyone who wanted to stay in federal service was able to do so, be it at the Marshal's Service, the Bureau of Prisons, or the administrative office of the courts, for example, and we helped those who didn't want to remain in the federal government locate in private industry.

Ironically, Congress has extended the life of the Parole Commission numerous times since then—most recently, the extension act of 2020 extended it until November 2022. As of this time, two commissioners comprise the body, including an acting chairman appointed by President George W. Bush and a commissioner appointed by President Barack Obama.

That meant general staff meetings over the years had a similar message. On July 19, 2006, I recounted the history of the Parole Commission to the staff as it existed when I was appointed and my original mandate to close it down by 1997. I then talked about taking over District of Columbia inmates when Lorton closed and those prisoners were absorbed into the federal system. That meant the Commission continued making parole decisions for old law DC parole eligible prisoners as well as for the supervision of prisoners sentenced after August 20000 in the Superior Court system of the District.

At that time the Commission was also beginning to inherit prisoners discharged from the Army and transferred from Fort Leavenworth's Disciplinary Barracks to the Federal Bureau of Prisons. That occurred when the military built a new, smaller prison. All these changes meant a dramatic change in the type of inmate in the system. There were both local violent crimes and major federal crimes. The Commission was more familiar with the federal crimes, and they also were the crimes for which our guidelines were crafted. A study had to be conducted to determine whether the guidelines as they existed actually reflected the local population. We also recommended an electronic management system and a victim coordinator position to aid in our work.

Though it was naïve to think we could predict what Congress would do, I knew it was imperative to continue to boost staff's morale. So I made sure I reiterated that I believed in the work we were doing and emphasized I knew that, under difficult circumstances, staff had been conscientious, cautious, and compassionate in the task of protecting the public. I made sure staff knew that long before I was part of the agency, the Commission had an excellent and distinguished record, which was testimony to their work. I wanted them to know that as long as I was part of the Commission, I would do my utmost to ensure each staff member would have a future. I, like them, wanted the agency to have more permanency, possibly extending responsibilities to the field of immigration or broadening supervision capability.

Peter Hoffman, chief of staff from 1995 through 1997, said in a May 2023 interview that I did several positive things to keep the existing staff engaged. "He was good at making connections, and that's what he loves to do," Hoffman said. "He was trying to keep things interesting for the staff who were there by providing educational experiences."

One example he mentioned was providing the opportunity for employees to learn how to use a defensive handgun. "A self-defense instructor came in 1995," Hoffman said. "It was a really good idea on his part, giving people the opportunity to learn new stuff. He wanted to hang on to good staff. Ed is not a micromanager. He'd leave his staff alone to get the day-to-day stuff done."

I encouraged all employees to share with senior staff what they believed could improve our services, as I believe if corporations or agencies aren't on the road to improvement, they'll be on the downhill slide. We all knew that the Parole Commission didn't have a high public profile unless we made a mistake and released the wrong person. In our day-to-day operations, we aimed to be an arm of law enforcement in removing from the streets those who posed a threat to that public safety.

I believe we had a stellar reputation within the parole arena, and it was my fervent desire to ensure that this reputation continued. If I left nothing else behind, I was determined to craft a reputation as a straight shooter and a person of integrity and character. I found myself exposed to many who didn't represent that philosophy, and I believe they dragged the agency down. But because of dedicated staff who carried on in spite of distractions and attempts to undermine the agency, we were able to overcome that. It proved to me that those who seek to do good eventually overcome those who have an agenda that isn't in the majority's best interests. Thus, I continued to believe the agency's future was bright as long as the team continued to work as a team.

Chief of Staff Hutchinson believed I took my work seriously, and he was correct. In a June 2023 interview, Hutchinson added, "He was not just signing papers, but he'd think about it until he felt he could reach the proper result. He knew he was dealing with people's jobs, concerns about the impact of the release on the victims and the people in the community, whether they might be frightened or scared, and how dangerous a potential parolee was apt to be."

Hearing Examiner Joe Pacholski, in a July 2023 interview, had this recollection: "Ed always wanted research done. He would implement research with the culture of the times. . . . If he was in charge, he was responsible and wanted the best possible answers for the time he was in charge."

In his role meeting directly with those eligible for parole, Pacholski said he particularly appreciated the fact that "Ed wanted us to do our jobs and call it the way we saw it. It is enormously rewarding when you know the head of the agency wants you to do your job and your decision shouldn't reflect on what he was going to do."

Overcrowding in federal correctional facilities hadn't previously been an issue. But incarcerating offenders, particularly those associated with committing drug offenses—such as crimes involving crack cocaine—ultimately led to a surge in federal prison populations. These offenders created an additional management problem. Many were nonviolent, but they were caught up in the system by virtue of the quantity of drugs in their possession. We saw a whole new group of offenders exposed to the real criminal professionals, many who had already been in prison for eons. These inmates, many coming from minority populations, learned quickly that in order to survive and fulfill their time, they had to answer to others.

This reminds me of the capital punishment issue and its application in society. I think the federal government has the tendency to inject itself into many issues over which it should have no oversight. I contend state governments should decide the appropriate sanctions for most crimes. For many decades, this was the predominant policy, and the right of the individual states was respected to establish penalties consistent with the thinking of their legislative and executive bodies.

Over a number of years, our federal lawmakers have reacted to public opinion as it regards some crimes (i.e., kidnapping, interstate transportation, illegal drug distribution) and have taken it upon themselves to usurp this authority from our states. The question of whether it has accomplished anything productive is open for debate. But we know that federalizing what were previously state crimes has led to a major influx in the federal prison population and the expansion of new prisons, to the tune of billions of dollars.

The Supreme Court has ruled on many criminal justice matters, including the application of capital punishment and its sentencing structures. In the opinion of Kennedy v. Louisiana, capital punishment cannot be inflicted unless a victim's life is taken. That being the case, states are free to exercise the prerogative of their legislative bodies in determining the appropriate sentence to which capital punishment would be applicable.

The 1984 abolishment of parole and establishment of United States sentencing guidelines was another example of federal intervention into the criminal justice system. We're now questioning these practices. We wonder if the structure has worked, or whether the abolishment of parole has served any useful purpose other than the creation of another federal bureaucracy. Has this changed anything impacting crime? That's a pertinent topic since we're on a new course of reducing sentences and directing United States attorneys not to pursue certain offenses to the full extent of the law. The question now is whether the states should be allowed to reestablish sensible, fair, and compassionate statutes that also recognize the rights of victims and the incarcerated.

As we look at our state criminal justice systems today, we see the application of many new innovative approaches that not only address the needs of offenders to rehabilitate, but also provide mentoring programs, educational opportunities, and mental and alcohol treatment programs. This is coupled with an emphasis on accepting responsibility for the offense committed through restitution to the victim and restorative justice.

12

Association of Parole Authorities International

I got still another education through my involvement with the Association of Paroling Authorities International, which consisted of more than forty parole agencies in the United States and American territories and ten countries, according to the 2019–2020 annual report. The federal Parole Commission was also represented at APAI training sessions, which involved sharing paroling policies other agencies adopted. It is a terrific organization, bringing all the key players to the table to consult and even adapt best practices they know work, or at least have benefited their agencies.

I served as the Northeast Regional vice chairman of the association, so I was able to share the success and practices the US Parole Commission used that were grounded guidelines based on a salient factor score. The result of years of research, the system provided a guide and road map to apply in making offenders' release decisions. Adopted in the late 1970s, this federal system was considered a model in parole release. Many of us on the Commission also used prayer, as we made decisions that significantly affected others' lives—not only the offender, but also the public. After all, our mission was protecting others from possible harm if we made the wrong decisions. We had those, but without the guideline system, there would have been a great many more.

Through that organization, I got to know some outstanding leaders in the field, some of whom remain good friends today. James Johnston is one of them. At that time, he was chairman of the military parole board for the Air Force. The military had different boards for the various branches of the military.

In an April 2023 interview, Johnston explained how we met and what benefits he saw in our international organization. "I ran into Ed at an annual chairmans' meeting," he said. "There were state chairs and also chairs of the four military boards. There were a chair or two from Canada, the United Kingdom, and New Zealand. The meeting was in Chicago, and I ran into Ed Reilly at Mass. I recognized him, and we went to dinner."

He believes the association "educated those attending on the established principles of what sociologists consider evidence to guide parole decisions."

The APAI also provided guidance on running a parole board, including who should serve on a board. Johnston said he attended the Department-of-Justice-funded training program, which APAI promoted. He recalls the APAI encouraged members to use professional guidelines to make decisions about paroling someone and dealing with violations. APAI also emphasized that state, military, and federal paroling authorities face the same issues. "Parole is part of the corrections rehabilitation process if it's well administered," Johnston contends.

He notes that I became part of APAI's executive council, part of four or five on the executive board, which pushed for improvements and the use of best practices in the parole process. "APAI had organizations that were like think tanks that provided the guidance and tried to explain the advantages of parole compared to determinant sentences. It was more productive and saved money, because using the guidelines you could efficiently pick those who should go back to prison," Johnston said.

"At Ed's urging, I organized meetings of the military boards and the Parole Commission," Johnston noted. "That's how I got to know him." He added, "Ed was a big deal in the Parole Commission. I will never forget how nice he is. As I've lived, there have been so many good things in society and he was one of them."

Johnston also elaborated on personal characteristics. "Ed was knowledgeable, thoughtful, and he was mature. I also got the feeling that, especially when he was chairman, he had two things: access to the attorney general, who would support him, and he knew some politicians who would support him. He wasn't running scared; he was doing the right thing."

When the paroling authorities got together, "He was the eight-hundred-pound gorilla," Johnston said. "They listened to him and followed his advice. Ed was pretty cagey about people and organizations, more than I would ever be."

I also initially met Cranston Mitchell through APAI when he was chairman of the Missouri Department of Corrections' board of probation and parole. President George W. Bush named Mitchell to the US Parole Commission in 2003.

"We were often in meetings together," Mitchell said in an April 2023 interview. "I enjoyed working with Ed, particularly when he was over the federal system and I was over the Missouri system. It was not uncommon for us to be on the same side of an argument. He provided a type of legitimacy; he carried himself in a way of importance, and it added greater professionalism to the organization and to the profession. He had an illustrious career, and I consider him a friend."

Mitchell believes APAI's efforts "were to move into a more scientific, data-filled future" for parole. The organization worked to inform and encourage paroling authorities to "look at the science, to look at the things being promoted." He added, "Ed, too, was a believer in utilizing science, to use a guideline matrix to assess whether [potential parolees] would be good citizens or poor risks."

Some parole board members "didn't necessarily have a public safety kind of background and weren't really suited for the role," Mitchell said. To counteract that, APAI published a book stressing the importance of governors setting in statute the qualifications to hold the position. Eventually most states set qualifications, and most governors seemed to understand the importance of the role.

Serving on a board, whether it's state or federal, can easily put you on the front page of newspapers and prominent in other media reports. Someone released might commit another sensational crime, or a parole official might succumb to the pressure of the promise of money or some other favor. There has always been debate about whether a parole official should be appointed as a political reward versus civil service employees. The onus is on the governor, and in my case, the president, to vet and make the ultimate decision about who should serve.

The law passed in 1939, during Franklin Roosevelt's administration, recognized parole was a result of what people felt the system needed. It was another way to review tough sentences of that era. Sound familiar?

We are at this point again with the current chaos we witness and the ongoing debate about how to handle those violating the law. Many consider the law venal because money or some other valuable consideration can curry favor. That's why some citizens feel those with money and position get different treatment in the criminal justice system.

This is why it's so critical to ensure those in the system act professionally and ethically. It's important that appointed executives are qualified and have a background that speaks to their qualifications. The system has come a long way, especially after the Association of Paroling Authorities International established guidelines that many states adopted. They should provide more confidence that "You only get justice if you buy it" is no longer the case.

The push for requirements to serve as parole board members was intended to prevent what had to be the "worst nightmare, what kept you up at night," Mitchell said, citing what he called the "Dukakis fiasco." Convicted murderer Willie Horton, who was serving life without parole, escaped during a weekend furlough and raped a woman and beat up and tied up her boyfriend. Michael Dukakis, a Massachusetts governor and presidential candidate, oversaw the furlough program. Mitchell explained, "You have to rely on good assessments and good tools in the toolbox to develop what you believe to be good solid public policy."

Another knowledgeable parole and correctional official I met through

APAI was Monica David Morris, who served as director of the organization for three years, beginning in 2015.

In an August 2023 interview, Morris said she met me when she attended her first APAI meeting as chairman of the Florida Parole Board. Her earlier extensive experience in the criminal justice field took place in Florida. In spite of all the improvements over the years, she said she would still like to see politics play less of a role in any criminal justice proceedings, including parole.

"For the future, I hope to see more fairness to criminals, less 'tough on crime' policies, better trained professionals working with criminals, and a modest approach to releases. I think if you believe in the parole process, you must believe in second chances for all," Morris said.

She said she's seen many successful parole cases, and she thinks more community corrections programs would make these even more likely, saving incarceration "for the deep-end cases who truly pose a danger to society." The mentally ill and criminally insane fall into that category.

Morris has nothing but praise for the APAI. "It [the agency's website] is a wealth of information, past and future. One must be careful in our line of work to not reinvent the wheel, and this organization is a very valuable tool as professionals to help us not do that."

She mentioned the media's relationship with parole officials, noting that it can be tricky, because their end product depends on their interpretation of what you've said. Morris fears the media is often more interested in the negative rather than the positive, so she found it was best "to employ a media spokesman who would be your buffer and keep you out of the fray."

I also met former US Parole Commissioner Michael Gaines at an APAI conference in Alabama. Gaines was chairman of Arkansas's state parole board at that time.

I promised at an APAI meeting at Lake Tahoe to summarize my public service and write of the impact APAI had on the fairness and equality that parole boards should deliver to those we oversee. It's our responsibility to help reform and return them to society. The Association of Paroling

Authorities International, dedicated to public safety, has played a critical role in bringing together parole officials dedicated to improvements. Using collaboration, communication, and training conferences, the goal was a more effective and fair system of releasing the incarcerated, while being ever mindful that the majority of those sentenced to prison will serve their time and be released.

Our responsibility extends to ensuring that those released have reformed and are prepared to reenter society. APAI has made commitments to achieve our mission and a few should be mentioned:

- We believe in the parole process as another option for reviewing sentencing that provides for a fairer justice system to enhance public safety.
- We want those given parole responsibility to have professional knowledge and be qualified before they are considered for appointment. After all, they have control over the lives of others.
- We are committed to lobby for development and improvement of rational parole practices and to educate our legislators about best practices.
- Always mindful of human dignity, we educate and demonstrate this philosophy to the community and to victims and offenders through the practices we employ.
- We never abandon the responsibility to interact with our United States and international partners to educate, learn, and share what other boards have learned in the course of their work. We have done this through successful training conferences.

Through sharing the success of the US Parole Commission guidelines that were a model, APAI members recognized the need to conduct research and implement a system within their own states. I believe the US Parole Commission, through its work and research, was the catalyst for many states to adopt their own guideline systems for their populations. Because of these partnerships and the Association, many paroling bodies have built a system that people feel is fair, based on what we learned as we made parole decisions.

APAI has an additional obligation, I believe, to further educate the public and the incarcerated on our mission and to learn how we might improve the delivery of what we offer. There is no question, however, that the role we have played has had a significant impact in most states, which has led to policies and guidelines resulting in a fairer parole process.

13

Why Parole?

Many of my colleagues, some who served with me on the Commission and others who oversaw the parole process at other levels, agree that the parole system has distinct advantages over determinant sentencing. Peter Hoffman, one of my earlier chiefs of staff, pointed to some parole history in a May 2023 interview. In the 1900s, either governors or wardens could release a prisoner or commute a sentence, but there were political risks to commutation.

At that time the major reasons for a parole board were cited as "rehabilitative programs that could help prisoners and reducing sentence disparity," because depending on whether a crime was committed in a rural or urban area, it could be considered more severe. "Finally, the parole board also got governors off the hook for someone who got out," Hoffman said. As the clock moved toward determinacy, Hoffman said, the argument became that there was more crime.

But he contends there were reasons for that. For one thing, the press had started covering crime more. The FBI director, J. Edgar Hoover, used a time clock in his presentations to Congress from 1950 to 1980. Keep in mind, the population increased during those years. It's little wonder his time clock showed a crime occurring every fifteen minutes, then every seven and a half minutes, and so on.

He understands the need to get rid of disparities, but Hoffman added, "I think it went further than it needed to. It makes sense to try to level the playing field, but that was one of the beauties of parole. You look at similarly situated people based on criminal behavior, and you need to look at the propensity to reoffend."

While some offenders participate in programs simply for appearances, "parole has the ability to engage that person, to explore how they view themselves," Hoffman said. Because drug or alcohol addiction is a lifelong obstacle, it's something that needs continued monitoring and support in the community. In the parole process, "you look for individuals who take advantage of opportunities to better themselves, becoming better citizens, addressing liabilities, staying out of difficulty," he believes. "That's part of why the benefits of parole are so advantageous versus the metrics involved in sentencing guidelines. It lacked the individual aspect for people. Everyone's road to criminal society is different, and the guidelines did not address that."

Former Commissioner Cranston Mitchell agrees. "Every case is unique. To have a cookie cutter approach is not the best public policy," nor does it support public safety. Often those who have earned parole can lead productive lives and move into the mainstream, Mitchell contends. "The ones we hear about are horrific, but many transition successfully."

Mitchell said the parole commissioners "use sophisticated data, look at a collection of criminals and look at some of the significant similarities (i.e., age of first crime, how far they've gone in school, what their employment history looks like, substance abuse difficulties, mental health), and weigh in on them as how low-risk or high-risk they might be."

James Johnston, who headed the Air Force Parole Board and was active in APAI, agrees that parole establishes principles based on sociological evidence. He points out a parole board could make exceptions if it looked at a sentence and it was outrageous for the crime (i.e., a hundred and fifty years). He also dislikes the mandatory minimum sentences often used in determinate sentencing. He thinks that's why prison populations increase, "and they don't work. They get the wrong person. They're used as bargaining chips." When Congress passed the legislation, "it applied to the smallest as well as the biggest cases, and the number of drug cases increased 60 percent," Johnston pointed out.

Former Commissioner Jasper Clay is also a staunch supporter of parole and has written an article against abolishing it. The paroling authority "knew better than the institution or the judges" when it comes to releases, he said. "We evaluated what the individual has done, his behavior in prison, and whether he's ready to become a productive citizen."

In making decisions, the commissioners could also take long sentences into account, in case a judge had imposed a particularly harsh sentence. "Parole commissioners could adjust the release so it would be earlier," Clay points out. Disciplinary situations in prison could also impact release times. A hearing examiner can also interact with the potential parolee, Clay said. There is also access to pre-sentence reports, criminal history, classification, what an inmate has achieved in prison, interaction with crime victims, as well as other factors—all of which provide evidence at to whether a potential parolee is a safe risk.

Chief of Staff Hutchinson sees the advantages and drawbacks to both parole and sentencing guidelines, but said he'd opt for parole. He contends that it's a fallacy to state that all judges will conform to the sentencing guidelines. But he also realizes parole can't take care of all disparities either. Parole, after all, can't ameliorate all problems because the convicted have to serve a minimum amount of time before they're parole-eligible.

But, as he points out, sentencing guidelines are imposed close to the event, so "you tend to miss what happens when that person is in prison." Besides, he notes, "Some people age out; they're simply too old to commit more crimes, and that can be identified more readily with parole."

Joe Pacholski, a hearing examiner for the Parole Commission beginning in 2000, observed in a July 2023 interview that he thought I viewed parole as a "second chance for most people, or a third; they had the chance to regain dignity and start life fresh." He remembers I took "great joy when an individual's termination hearing" occurred, which meant they were released from supervision. I remember we used to think if someone could survive the first three months without reoffending, they had at least a decent chance of making it.

Pacholski believed "Ed thought [the termination hearings] were the success stories for him, because he got them broken, and by the time the hearings were done, people were restored back to where they were." That was a goal, as was closing down the Parole Commission. He thought I must have recognized the importance of the Parole Commission, because if I'd closed it down in the allotted time I'd been given, I would have had a good chance at an ambassadorship to Ireland, a post I'd sought earlier. Actually, I thought I might come back to Kansas and run for governor.

But obviously that was not to be, as we got more and more cases—some from DC when Lorton closed, some from the military, who transferred a number of parole-eligible prisoners from the old disciplinary barracks at Fort Leavenworth when a new, smaller one was constructed. We also were in charge of witness protection cases. Former Commissioner Mitchell elaborated on some of those cases, noting the Commission "made decisions that judges would generally make. If someone was in witness protection, they were not given a prison sentence, but they were given probation. We had the ability to revoke that probation if they chose not to comply."

Their files had to be kept in a locked environment, and the Commission had to use extreme discretion and sensitivity in handling them. The files were always hand-carried, Mitchell said. Those in witness protection could easily put themselves at risk even though they're given a new identity. In many cases, they had been involved in organized crime. If their probation was revoked, there was caution in working out reciprocity details. For example, they might go to a state prison to serve the remaining sentence rather than a federal facility, where they'd be more at risk.

14

My Mentors

October 21, 2011, was the day to highlight a "Salute to the Leader," Senator Bob Dole, a loyal supporter of mine over the years. Likewise, I supported Dole in his campaigns for the Senate and presidency. As the senator addressed the group, I noticed an uncanny similarity in the ways our careers in public service paralleled. He started as assistant Russell County attorney, and when he was working late in his office, a fellow Republican approached him. The Russell County Republicans needed somebody to run for public office who would burn the midnight oil. That was the beginning of Bob Dole's service in the Kansas State Legislature.

My career began after my University of Kansas graduation, when I returned to Leavenworth and associated with Reilly & Sons as a realtor and insurer. As I met our clients, I was encouraged to think about running for public office. It was 1963 when a former county attorney, James Fussell, also decided to seek the House of Representatives seat being vacated by Robert Behee. I decided to challenge him for the position, and thanks to the GOP precinct men and women, I was successful. That was the beginning, followed by twenty-eight more years as a Kansas senator and nearly nineteen in Washington, DC, as a presidential appointee.

I've always had the utmost respect for Senator Dole, not only for his illustrious career in public service, but for many other reasons. He exemplified not only public service, but sacrifice during World War II. Dole received two Purple Hearts and a Bronze Star with "V" device for his attempt to assist a downed radioman during his service. The injuries left him with limited mobility in his right arm and numbness in his left arm. Those injuries affected him the rest of his life, and it makes you wonder how a public servant could succeed in that situation. But he proved you can, through determination as well as love and compassion for others and a strong desire to serve. Dole's life is the story of a small-town Kansas boy working at a soda fountain in his hometown of Russell who definitely made good. He became one of the most successful and loyal Americans to serve in the United States Congress. He served in the United States House for eight years and in the United States Senate for more than twenty-seven years.

His commitment to this country is apparent in his three attempts to become president of the United States. He got the bid from the GOP only once to run for that office, in 1996, when he was defeated by William Jefferson Clinton. Though Dole didn't succeed in this quest, he continued to serve with distinction and became well known for his ability to bring compromise and good will to the congressional negotiating table. He and others, like Senator Tip O'Neill—longtime speaker of the House from Massachusetts, known for working on both sides of the aisle—were masters at treating others with respect while recognizing that to get anything done in a deliberating body, you must project good will, civility, character and moral integrity.

Neither played what I call the blame game—finding excuses why something couldn't be done. Rather, they carried out the memorable words of John Fitzgerald Kennedy: "Ask not what your country can do for you, ask what you can do for your country." Dole never stopped trying to bring civil discourse to the debate, and he was successful with both his Republican and Democratic colleagues. That is why he will be remembered in the annals of American history. The leadership both Dole and O'Neill brought to Congress speaks for itself by the successes they enjoyed. And the American people were the beneficiaries of their service.

The Dole Institute at the University of Kansas is another example of

Senator Bob Dole's effort to challenge this nation not only to preserve history, but also to bring back civil discourse and respect to the public square. America has the unique ability to recover from many challenges, including wars, disasters, and health crises like COVID-19. We can turn the course we are on and return to civility if we focus on serving one another in the way Senators Bob Dole and Tip O'Neill did. The Golden Rule is another place to start as we face the United States' current challenges.

My association over many years with Senator Bob Dole and my admiration of his service prompted me to establish the Edward F. Reilly Public Engagement Fund at my alma mater, the University of Kansas. This is an effort to encourage other men and women to make the sacrifice and enter the public square. Some of the engagement funds have also been extended to the Dole Institute. The Institute is doing its part to educate students about the importance of public service as they recognize the obligation we all have to use our skills, education, and wisdom to secure the peace, prosperity, and freedom our constitutional authors envisioned.

My support offers the opportunity for career professionals and other public servants to share their knowledge with students. It's also my way of acknowledging how grateful I am for the support I received from those who served. Even in my early days of legislative service, I had many mentors, two of whom stood out prominently: State Representative John Gardner of Johnson County, who mentored me in the House, as well as Representative and future Congressman Keith Sebelius.

It was Sebelius who brought a class of twenty-four state senators on one of our first trips to Washington, putting us up at the later notorious Watergate Hotel, where Senator and Elizabeth Dole lived. Sebelius's daughter-in-law, Kathleen, became governor of Kansas and secretary of Health and Human Services under President Barack Obama. Coincidentally, Kathleen Sebelius and I served in the Kansas House and Senate at the same time. She was the chairman of the House Federal and State Affairs Committee, and since I was her counterpart in the Senate, we often worked together. Her father-in-law, a congressman, was one of the state's most illustrious representatives.

Nancy Landon Kassebaum was another great friend and Kansas statesman, the first woman to represent Kansas in the US Senate. Politics had been a part of Nancy's life since her father, Alf Landon, served two terms as governor from 1933–1937. He was the 1936 GOP political candidate. She was well known for her ability to build coalitions with her practical approach to issues facing the country. She served from 1978 through 1997.

Her father introduced me to many of his friends when I was candidate for the US Congress in 1974. On a number of occasions, I was a guest of Governor Landon, who loved Irish whiskey, along with Lew Ferguson of the Associated Press. We sat in his library and discussed the political environment and some of the challenges we faced in Kansas. What a privilege to be included in these fireside chats!

Nancy predicted in remarks at the Dole Institute at the University of Kansas that in today's political environment, she could not be elected—a sentiment I shared. As moderates, I would have to concede that many of us wouldn't be acceptable to our parties today.

Another special day for me occurred in October 2006. Visiting with two presidents in one week doesn't happen under normal circumstances. The first instance provided an opportunity to express my appreciation to President Bill Clinton as we honored him with the National Law Enforcement Leadership Award.

That week I also attended the Republican Senatorial Committee luncheon at the Mayflower Hotel with President George Bush and Senators Elizabeth Dole and Mitch McConnell. As I had my picture taken, I expressed thanks for chance to serve with Bush 43. President Clinton is always quick with a response and noted, "If you're still around through three presidents, then you must be doing something right as a Republican." President Bush said, "I haven't read about the US Parole Commission, so you must be doing OK. Keep up the good work."

Two days later, I was in the Department of Justice meeting a bunch of the new US attorneys who had just been appointed to their posts. It was a moving ceremony as Attorney General Alberto Gonzalez gave them the charge and wished them well. I stuck around to congratulate them, but they all seemed so young.

Another close friend and ally from my DC days was Katja Bullock, who had worked for President Reagan as well as George H. W. and George W. Bush. She also worked for governors of Maryland in championing appointments of qualified individuals. She was recently acknowledged by former Governor Larry Hogan for her service in so many administrations, including his own.

The association with Commissioner John Simpson was another blessing when I was the new guy. John had served as director of the Secret Service from 1981 to 1992. He retired prior to the election of George H. W. Bush, who knew John and had the wisdom to appoint him to the US Parole Commission. When I arrived nine months later in 1992, we were fortunate to have a group of professional and well-equipped commissioners. John knew where every foxhole and minefield was in the nation's capital, and he was a great mentor for me, as he helped show me where to step. Though he'd served only nine months before I came, he had absorbed all the insides and outsides of the Commission and was helpful in my transition as chairman.

I am blessed to have so many who played an important part in my life. It's impossible to name all of them, but I was always ready to accept the counsel and support of those who believed I could do the job. That paid off in dividends since those who had confidence in my abilities stayed with me throughout my public service. I had the opportunity to meet both George Reed and Ben Baer, previous chairmen of the federal board. I was able to absorb some of the philosophy and advice they both had to share. Reed was the longest serving chairman of the US Parole Commission, holding that position for nineteen years. He was vice chairman for an additional six years.

15

Sex, Scandal, and Lies

Despite the positive mission of the Parole Commission, the agency became a victim of those who sought power as commissioners and ultimately wanted to establish themselves as the leader of the agency. This was the situation that developed during my tenure when a new commissioner was sworn in. That commissioner made numerous attempts to unseat me as the presiding chairman.

My time at the office became a daily game that finally concluded in the resignation of that commissioner and the eventual overthrow of the chairman. This occurred through accusations, innuendos, lies, and possibly sexual misdeeds. As a student of government and a long-serving legislator, none of this came as a surprise to me, as it exists in many work situations today. It was extremely disappointing since the majority of our commissioners were true professionals dedicated to the public good; most wanted only to fulfill the mission of the agency, which had so much power over the lives of others and the time they served in prison.

I knew that entering public service wanting to accomplish something good doesn't shield you from those who want to defeat you because they want your job or they want someone else in your job. Politics affects public service in a variety of ways. The appointment process is one. Someone may dig up any bad thing you've ever done—or that they think you've done. Your background has to be squeaky clean, or you have to figure out how you will handle things in your past that can be used against you.

That happened to my dad, who wanted to serve on the Water Board. Opponents claimed he only wanted to serve to get a line run to his farm. It wasn't true, but it cost him the appointment. If there is nothing people can hold against you, they will make it up. Later, my father ran for mayor and was elected by a wide margin and was reelected to a second term. He decided not to run for a third term.

Unfortunately, in government service, what can transpire is an effort by others to advance themselves at any cost, regardless of your civil service status—especially if you're a political appointee. This is all the more reason not to give them the opportunity, and it demonstrates why you must have loyal senior staff. A good friend of mine who is a competent attorney held the position of US pardon attorney, but he was sabotaged by a creative employee who wanted the top job. I endured a similar situation.

My experience was initiated by an attractive young woman who had been an assistant district attorney in California. Ironically, when she was to be sworn in, her father said, "Reilly, keep her out of trouble like she was in California." Unfortunately, she had allies internally in the Department of Justice and in the White House whom she enlisted in her efforts. She had not been with the Commission long when it became apparent to staff what she was doing and the disruption she introduced to the orderly process of the office.

In a June 2023 interview, Chief of Staff Thomas Hutchinson called her a "subversive character who had been working at the White House. I thought the White House had been unfair with Ed, because she was a problem in California." He estimated she served on the Commission for possibly two and a half years.

It turns out the theft of some of my files at the office was a scam. Security officials figured out this commissioner and her boyfriend, who later became her husband, had entered the office, got my spiral notebook and copied pages from my files. Her boyfriend, an assistant US district attorney, was starting a file on me. I had written a letter to the Department of Transportation about the need for improvements on the Route 92 highway from Missouri because of the traffic to the Leavenworth penitentiary,

Fort Leavenworth, and the Eisenhower VA Medical Center. They claimed I shouldn't have used Commission stationery to do this, and they got a copy of it. The pair also alleged the Reillys owned property in Missouri, which we didn't.

Hutchinson said the files were "spirited away," and it turned out she had "burgled his office." He contends the problem was she was "trying to run the Commission in a way he didn't want it to go." Hutchinson hoped to get the support of one of the other commissioners to put a stop to this, but that didn't happen.

When I asked the Office of Inspector General to look into the file theft, the agents talked to all the commissioners except her. She was deliberately avoiding them, claiming she had appointments or meetings or otherwise wasn't available. They finally confronted her. She subsequently resigned from the Parole Commission and became a divorce lawyer.

Hutchinson recalled she "disappeared during the investigation," but ultimately admitted to the theft. Under pressure from the attorney general and the White House, she resigned. He called it a "bad time" and one when the "atmosphere wasn't very good," when "normally the Commission was very collegial."

Her boyfriend came to my apartment building as part of an effort to stalk me. Two residents saw him slip through the door opened by security and asked him what he was doing. He told them he was visiting, but he wouldn't give a name and didn't know what floor he was going to. They called 911, and he quickly left.

The two eventually married, but sometime later, her husband was seeking a divorce and called me to make a statement. I referred him to my attorney. Hutchinson also recalls her husband calling me looking for information to use during the proceedings. Some of the Commission's analysts told me she'd been having an affair with another analyst. She often visited his office, and they always closed the door.

She later called and said she needed to talk to me. I asked her what about, and she insisted she had to talk to me in person. I told her I'd meet her at a nearby large restaurant, and I made sure it was at a table near other patrons. I asked her outright if she'd copied my files. She said something about "We." She never actually admitted it, but I knew she had.

So I failed in my promise to her father to keep her out of trouble, as she brought her fair share of trouble to the process and the agency. The accusations she made about me were untrue, and the Department of Justice was embarrassed by the whole experience. I gladly retired after that year to spend more time with my teenage son. It was a definite reminder of something I knew about all appointees: You must always watch your back, as there are always those trying to crawl the ladder and bring you down.

Many who choose to seek federal office are naïve and unaware that they're putting their name and family in the bullseye. This is both because of the public scrutiny and also the investigation by federal officials such as the FBI or other intelligence agencies. Even your neighbors and friends may suddenly find it necessary to bring up an old beef they had with you. In other words, it's a great opportunity to sink whatever you're trying to accomplish, and in the process, wreck and humiliate yourself and family who you pray will forgive you.

And we wonder why many good, professional, well-qualified Americans are not rushing to file for office. Many ask that question as we enter another political season and they fret over the candidates and incumbents, since they're dissatisfied with their choices. Politics is definitely not for the faint-hearted and never has been. Yet it's a critical part of our experiment that created a constitutional system that guarantees the right to life, liberty, and the pursuit of happiness. Those chosen to serve have the opportunity to represent those who put their trust in them by casting their most precious gift, their vote. That should never be violated by those seeking personal gain, reward, and recognition.

I was fortunate to get through my years of service without ruining my name and that of my family, in spite of efforts to tarnish both my name and service. Climbers are always scaling the ladder to replace the guy ahead of them by whatever means. Competition is great, but those who use ulterior motives in efforts to sabotage another's career should be called to the altar of retribution.

16

History of the Parole Commission

I've always believed it's important to know our history, because if we don't know where we've been, it's hard to tell where we're going. This is just as true of criminal justice as anything else. That's why I want to summarize the development of the parole release system for federal prisoners from its inception in 1910 to its termination by the Sentencing Reform Act of 1984. I think this provides a useful example of how sentencing and corrections have changed over the years and what we may learn from such change.

In the United States, parole first saw the light of day at the Elmira Reformatory in New York, shortly before the turn of the century. Prior to that, the sentence handed down by the court was served in full, unless it was pardoned or commuted. Pardoning meant forgiveness; if the sentence was commuted, it amounted to an act of mercy. The results were sometimes startling. John Wesley Hardin, the gunfighter with probably the highest body count, was pardoned after his fortieth killing on the grounds of rehabilitation. Blue Duck—for your history buffs, he was one of Belle Starr's husbands—was pardoned after serving a year of a federal homicide life sentence.

Federal offenders were allowed good time, a sentence reduction that varied through the years from 1867 to 1987, which was a precursor of parole. However, good time failed to address some concerns (e.g., unduly harsh sentences imposed shortly after the crime, disparity in sentencing, prison overcrowding, the need for rehabilitative efforts and rewards for positive behavior, and the need for post-release supervision).

In 1910, the federal system joined many state systems in adopting parole. The prisoner was eligible for parole after serving a third of the sentence, and those released on parole remained on post-release supervision until the end of the sentence. If denied, the prisoner was released at the end of the sentence minus good time. The legislation established a parole board at each of the three major federal prisons. In 1930, Congress created a full-time, centralized US Board of Parole in Washington, DC.

In the late 1930s and early 1940s, Congress was again concerned with sentence disparity and proposed the court impose the maximum sentence; four months later, the parole board would hear the case and set a presumptive release date, which could later be modified. This legislation is similar to the system of decision guidelines and presumptive parole dates that the US Parole Commission implemented administratively in the 1970s. In the 1970s, the Attica prison riot occurred, and Congress started hearings on the need to reform the federal parole system. At the same time, the Commission was involved in a grant-funded project that created parole decision-making guidelines used in the federal parole system for more than two decades.

These guidelines were organized in a two-dimensional grid. The vertical axis shows an offense score with eight categories. Category 8 contains the most serious offenses, including murder and kidnapping, and Category 1 the least serious offenses, such as larceny of $2,000 or less. On the horizontal axis is the salient factor score. This includes the number of prior convictions and commitments, age, probation or parole status, time free since last commitment, and heroin dependence, ranging from zero to ten points. High scores indicate a high likelihood of recidivism, low scores a low likelihood.

At the intersection of the two dimensions is the guideline range in months. To get that, you have to determine the offense score and calculate the salient factor score, which will result in the guideline range. Aggravating and mitigating factors can be considered in departures from guidelines. There's also a separate guideline to punish serious disciplinary infractions and guidelines to reward superior prison program achievement. These guideline systems represent a balance between rule and discretion, and over the years, 80 to 90 percent of all parole decisions have been within the guideline ranges.

At the time, Congress favored the guidelines and incorporated them in the Parole Commission and Reorganization Act of 1976. This is when the Board of Parole was renamed the Parole Commission. Meanwhile, various states had begun to abolish parole, either replacing it with large amounts of good time or developing sentencing guidelines.

Federal sentencing guidelines also hit the scene in the late 1960s with the Brown Commission Report, ultimately resulting in legislation to create a Sentencing Commission to write them. The US Parole Commission and parole guidelines were to be replaced by this new system. The main argument was that it would be more effective than parole guidelines in reducing disparity because it would reach all sentencing decisions, not just the imprisonment decisions. It was also believed to provide "truth in sentencing" because the sentence served would be determinate—the sentence imposed by the court less 15 percent good time.

During the late 1970s and early 1980s, Congress discussed these ideas but couldn't agree, so nothing was enacted. But in 1984, two things happened. First, the major criminal code reform effort was abandoned. Second, the sentencing provisions—including sentencing guidelines, parole abolition, and reduction of good time—were detached and made a separate bill. Known as the Sentencing Reform Act of 1984, this eventually became law in the waning days of the term as part of budget resolution, thus avoiding the normal process. This meant a major provision of the original reform act never passed—reducing statutory maximum penalties by one third to take into account the abolition of parole and reduction of good time.

The voting members of the Sentencing Commission were appointed at the end of 1985. By statute, the attorney general and the chair of the Parole Commission are ex officio, nonvoting members of the Sentencing

Commission. The new guidelines took effect on November 1, 1987, and they apply to every federal offender whose crime was committed on or after that date.

So what has been the result? Unfortunately, mandatory minimum sentences and sentencing guidelines don't mesh well in practice. In fact, a Senate report to the Sentencing Reform Act of 1984 specifically highlights their incompatibility. Nonetheless, the two systems now exist side by side, and Congress—intending to show its toughness on crime—adds to the list of mandatory minimum sentences almost every year.

Initially, the Sentencing Commission guidelines were much more complicated than those of the Parole Commission, apparently to satisfy the intent of Congress. However, eight years later, the Sentencing Commission was in the middle of a major effort to simplify its guidelines. This would make them more closely resemble the federal parole guidelines.

The concept of parole supervision still exists but is now called supervised release. Judges, rather than the parole board, conduct revocation hearings, though some judges have begun to wonder if there is a way of relieving them of some of this workload. So what has happened to the Parole Commission?

It still exists to handle prisoners serving sentences for crimes committed prior to November 1, 1987, but it's being downsized administratively. The Commission will need to exist for some time, though, to accommodate the "old law" cases either in prison or on parole supervision. Most are violent or otherwise serious offenders serving extremely long sentences. The Commission has been extended frequently by legislation.

So what have we learned? We can see that sentencing and correctional legislation is somewhat cyclical—to some extent we continue to reinvent the wheel. This is clearly the case with mandatory minimum sentences. But at the same time, we're making some progress. I'm sure there will continue to be tension between determinate and indeterminate sentences, between sentencing and discretion, and between mandatory minimums and guidelines, just as there has always been. Whether we've seen the final balance remains to be seen.

Most interestingly, although the Parole Commission is being phased out, the major concepts the Commission developed have all taken root in the federal criminal justice system: post-release supervision, structured decision-making using explicit guidelines, incorporation of an empirical prediction instrument, and the provision of due process by written reasons for decisions and an appellate review system. I am an optimist; although there will be setbacks, I believe over time we have a good chance of making the criminal justice system both fairer and more effective. And that's why I think it's so important that we know our history.

17

Where Do We Go from Here?

The abolition of parole in 1984 by the United States Congress led us from an indeterminate parole system to a determinate sentencing model of "Do the crime and you will do the time." That philosophy, though beginning to mellow, is still a part of the federal criminal justice system. Efforts to change sentencing structure are in the forefront of today's political landscape.

During my nearly eighteen years as an ex officio member of the United States Sentencing Commission, I observed the evolution of federal sentencing policy firsthand. As a former Kansas state senator and a United States Parole commissioner, I am also acquainted with the previous indeterminate system that served states and the federal government for decades. In the past thirty years or more, many states, following the lead of the federal system, have replaced the traditional authority once reserved for paroling authorities to grant early release to deserving inmates followed by a lengthy period of community supervision. Since 1984, when Congress approved determinate sentencing, many states have also replaced the traditional release authority with a similar determinate structure. This results in structured sentencing guidelines in an effort to reduce sentencing disparity.

What I've learned is that about every three decades, we review the system in place, and it often returns to the previous approach. In truth, the options are limited and attempting to develop the best practices implemented by either states or the federal government seems to offer the greatest likelihood of success.

Once again we find ourselves in this situation as we strive to address the issue of offenders returning to their communities. Once again we have an opportunity to address the issue of whether our current criminal justice system is meeting its obligation not only to punish, but to rehabilitate the offender. This is possible if we provide the opportunity for vocational training and treatment while the offender is incarcerated so they may then become a productive member of society.

So what have we learned? Research has shown that a longer period of incarceration doesn't, in most cases, result in lower recidivism. Often it results in a more dangerous individual who has had lengthy exposure to the harsh realities of prison life.

Prison life is not for the faint of heart, as I learned during my service in corrections as a legislator and parole commissioner. It's not just a question of doing time for your crime; it could include more unpleasant punishment such as assault or rape. It could even mean self-mutilation, which many do just to go to the hospital for treatment, if they can. One warden at Kansas State Penitentiary decided he wouldn't respond to any future cutting of the Achilles tendon with outside treatment. To discourage that conduct, an inmate was shipped to the prison infirmary, where surgery was performed without anesthesia.

Some inmates tried to serve their sentences minding their own business, only to realize there are bullies who want to dominate others by assault or sexual gratification. Others were placed in solitary confinement for their own protection, or because they violated prison rules, or even because they went on a hunger strike. Whatever the reason, it's not what we're trying to accomplish as rehabilitation. I know judges trying to fulfill the oath they have taken are not as informed as they should be about prison life. They don't realize every person they sentence to prison should be evaluated. The Justice Department has appointed masters or reviewers at many state prisons because of reports of mismanagement and internal problems. Often inmates conduct hunger strikes to protest prison conditions and sometimes just to raise hell and make life miserable for those not participating. Solitary confinement is no assurance that you won't be subject to an attack in your cell, since sometimes others manage to get into a locked cell that's meant to protect those in witness protection.

Consider the recent case in West Virginia where organized crime boss James "Whitey" Bulger was transferred between facilities, and bets were placed on how long he would last in his new location. As it turned out, the eighty-nine-year-old Bulger, who was in failing health, was bludgeoned to death with a padlock less than twelve hours after arriving at the prison in Hazelton in 2018. This is another example that the Justice Department's inspector general labeled mismanagement or a deliberate attempt to eliminate an inmate. Bulger was in a Florida prison for years after a 2013 conviction for murders and racketeering, and there was no good reason to move him, considering his career and his testimony against others engaged in criminal activity. As the prison grapevine goes, the Hazelton inmates knew he was coming, and because he'd been a government informant, he didn't have a chance.

This incident added to a list of troubles facing the Bureau of Prisons, which has struggled recently with misconduct, staff shortages, and other issues. I don't recall these issues occurring when the BOP was directed by Norman Carlson and Kathleen Hawk, who were exceptional leaders. Director Carlson, the fourth head of the BOP, started his career at the US Penitentiary in Leavenworth.

One of government's most critical missions is to provide everyone the ability to enjoy life and raise a family without fear of becoming a crime victim. But as we witness what has happened on our streets in major metropolitan areas, crime will continue to be a major issue in every election. If people can't rely on their government to provide that constitutional right, then the government has failed at its number one obligation. Public safety will definitely be on the front burner moving forward. Radical and uniformed groups have assaulted law enforcement, put merchants out of business, and forced major stores to move or close. They've attacked people of all ages and status. This is not the America we know. Our judicial system should protect the public, meting out punishment against those who break the law while protecting the rights ensured by the rule of law. America's open borders have become another major issue. A country can't maintain its identity or peace on its streets if immigration laws aren't enforced.

Many who determine what should happen in the criminal justice system aren't well informed. Most haven't been actively engaged in the work of any of these agencies. This leads to much misunderstanding about what really occurs in day-to-day operations. The discontent we now witness in law enforcement, resulting in slower reactions and problems in correctional institutions, comes from lack of support and recognition of how important these agencies are.

Problems are often exacerbated because the determinate system causes a major increase in our prison populations, consisting mainly of low-level offenders who need drug treatment and counseling. Abolishing discretionary early release for deserving offenders has resulted in overcrowding in state and federal systems. This results in huge costs to taxpayers, who have previously cut funds needed for education and social programs in the prisons.

The United States is now the number one incarcerator in the world, and it doesn't have the programs necessary for those who need rehabilitation. In both state and federal systems that have abolished indeterminate sentencing, prisoners don't have a great incentive to turn their lives around because they know it won't be rewarded. Thirty years ago, we saw inmates anxious to participate in prison programs and to abide by the rules.

Current policy, once popular with voters, is changing as many states return to a form of traditional release discretion with post-release supervision. The United States Sentencing Commission has recognized the need to address the disparities caused by some sentencing laws—such as sanctions for the distribution of crack cocaine—while seeking alternatives for certain low-level offenders. Data accumulated over the period of determinate sentencing tell us we need a total review of the criminal justice system and the federal code. This must focus on treatment for those in need, coupled with a sensible release policy by well-qualified parole or equivalent release authority. Reentry must be the focus in releasing offenders, with mentors available to assist, support, and monitor those who return to society.

As we reflect on what lies in the future, I recognize that every two to three decades, there are really no new approaches but instead a restructuring of policies. Consider community policing, which used to entail a man or a woman on the beat; it has returned years later, with officers on bikes and Segways.

I believe in the concept of parole. I remember the thoughtfulness with which the Commission went over the offenders' files and conducted the hearings. What we looked for was remorse, including willingness to make restitution and admission of their guilt, among other things.

I don't believe there will be another parole board, as such, but there probably will be another agency in charge of release mechanisms with guidelines similar to the parole board. Peter Hoffman, who was tasked with writing the Parole Commission guidelines, was later asked to craft guidelines for the Sentencing Commission, and I noticed how similar they are. He said yes, he'd tweaked the old guidelines to create the new set.

What can we expect to happen in criminal justice and corrections in the next thirty years? Here are some of my predictions:

1. A more compassionate approach to long, determinate sentencing with no opportunity for review.
2. Excuses for overcrowding in some institutions.
3. An experimentation with drug leniency, which, in the words of Dr. Menninger, can potentially lead to the use of stronger drugs.
4. Reduced sentences for minor drug offenders, which, in my opinion, should be a matter of debate.
5. A continued struggle and debate over the use of capital punishment in the most serious cases, such as premeditated murder. I think this debate fails to acknowledge that sentencing a

person to life for serious crime doesn't eliminate the threat posed to those working in a dangerous prison environment. For them, capital punishment can be a severe management tool for acts committed while the offender is incarcerated.

With all that said, I predict we will eventually see a more lenient approach, which will be another experiment in human control of other humans to live, respect, and abide by the laws. Only time will tell if the experiment is innovative and successful. Hopefully, lawmakers will have the foresight and judgment to ask what we have learned thus far that might have a positive impact on human behavior. This could include restorative justice, successful mentor programs, restitution, community corrections, and supervised release.

We should have learned by now that educating the press and public is a full-time job for those engaged in legislation and reforming the criminal justice system. It is crucial if we are to enlist the families of offenders and the leaders of society. They need to realize that parole is just one mechanism to protect society and a method for evaluating an offender through good time and institutional behavior before release. But those who are released will face problems with employment, hostile neighborhoods, and the shame of family and friends. Frankly, it may be more than they can endure, tempting them to return to the previous life of crime. The education never ceases if we are to recognize that it will take community, industrial leaders, directors of personnel, and our social agencies to cushion this traumatic experience of reentering society.

I have discovered a few current programs designed with reentry and second chances in mind. The November 2023 edition of *The Beacon*, a newspaper published in Silver Spring, Maryland that reaches greater Washington, DC, ran a story about Georgetown University's Prison Scholars program, which is part of its Prisons and Justice Initiative. Marc Howard, the founding director of the initiative that helps prisoners earn college degrees and offers assistance after they're released, was motivated to start this program after helping a high school friend who was wrongly convicted for his father's murder. The friend, Marty Tankleff, was exonerated after seventeen years in prison. As part of the initiative, Howard and Tankleff co-teach a class at Georgetown called "Making an Exoneree."

Neil Roland teaches world affairs in the District of Columbia's jail through this program. He has also tutored prisoners at a maximum security prison at Jessup, Maryland, for eight years.

In addition to this initiative, Marc Howard also founded the Frederick Douglass Project for Justice, aimed at encouraging those in the free world to come to prisons to meet and engage with prisoners. He wants those on the outside to realize that incarcerated people share a common humanity with them.

18

Public and Private Life Intersect

Sometimes what happens because of our public lives has a great bearing on our private lives. At least I have found that to be true in my life. Because I grew up in Leavenworth, I have always been aware of the adjoining Fort Leavenworth and the Command and General Staff College. I didn't know that it would become an important part of my life, even though I was never a member of the military.

One of my mentors, Kansas US Senator Bob Dole, often said, "If it's happening in America, it usually happened first in Kansas." The city of Leavenworth is an example of that, going back to the establishment at Fort Leavenworth of the International Officers Association. This dates back to 1881, when General William T. Sherman established the school for infantry and cavalry. Thirteen years later our first officer from Switzerland, Henri LeComte, attended classes at Fort Leavenworth. The last report I know of, published in 1993, listed more than 5,500 officers from 122 countries who were Leavenworth graduates.

This program has resulted in great friendships and allies for America which can influence relationships with other countries to ensure peace. During my career, I welcomed each year's international class to the Kansas Legislature. Later I was asked to conduct lectures at the fort introducing the components of our local, county, state, and federal governments. As a sponsor for the Irish officers, I have developed lasting friendships with many families over the years, and I still maintain contact with them.

These are the Irish Defense officers I got to know during the years I was in Leavenworth:

Colonel and Mrs. Colin Campbell; General and Mrs. Con Cream; Commandant and Mrs. Michael Gannon; General and Mrs. Eddie Heskin; Commandant and Mrs. Sean McCann; General and Mrs. Gerry McMahon; General and Mrs. William O'Dwyer; Commandant and Mrs. Brian McKevitt; Commandant and Mrs. Paul Pakenham; Colonel Denis Parsons and wife; Commandant and Mrs. Con Ryan; Lieutenant General and Mrs. D. F. Stapleton; General and Mrs. Desmond Swan; and Commandant and Mrs. John Durmin.

Because of these associations, I had the opportunity to land on the USS John F. Kennedy warship on its first port of call to Ireland. The experience holds a special spot in my memory, as this was the first time a United States warship had been allowed in an Irish port. One of the officers I sponsored, General Sean McCann, arranged for my flight to board the ship prior to its docking in the port.

I was taken from the Dublin airbase, landing on the JFK as it approached the port of Dublin. The warship landed at Dún Loahgaire. I shall never forget the experience, as it reminded me of my annual chiropractic adjustment when we hit the deck.

The visit brought much excitement to Ireland in view of the Kennedy family association. I visited with Jean Kennedy Smith, who was the ambassador at the time. As I reflect on my Irish American roots, regardless of politics, this was a special time in life to celebrate JFK for his service to our nation and the challenge that still rings in our memory, "My fellow Americans, ask not what your country can do for you, ask what you can do for your country."

Years later, in 2004, I was one of twenty-five recruited to escort Cardinal George of Chicago to France for the sixtieth anniversary of the landing at Omaha Beach. The day was moving for those of us present on the beach, as it included Mass at the American cemetery celebrated by the Cardinal and assisted by none other than Cardinal Joseph Ratzinger. Some months later he became Pope Benedict the XVI. During our visit

I had the opportunity to dine with the Cardinal, who was a gracious and humble servant of Christ. As I reflect on his passing, I realize he was the right man for the job. During his tenure, he was a progressive who recognized the importance of taking a conservative approach to modification of Catholic doctrine and history. He will be remembered for the compassionate leadership of 1.1 billion Catholics from 2005 to 2013. I shall always remember the night I had dinner across the table from this gracious gentleman who became Christ's representative.

It was obvious at this solemn service that the powers of the church did not want the president of the United States in attendance, considering the request for the US Ambassador to the Holy See to attend, because of the president's views on abortion rights and gay marriage that run counter to those of the Vatican.

On a lighter note, I had the privilege of meeting Irish actress Maureen O'Hara at the White House during the Reagan years, when I was one of the candidates for ambassador of Ireland. I'd been recommended by Senator Dole and others. An editorial in *The Kansas City Times* on March 9, 1981, noted that President Reagan might name a "widely known Irishman from this area, Sen. Edward F. Reilly Jr., a Kansas state senator, as the US ambassador to Ireland."

The editorial went on to say, "Republican U.S. Sen. Bob Dole and Nancy Landon Kassebaum of Kansas; Mayor Richard L. Berkley, long active in Republican politics; Mayor Jack Reardon of Kansas City, Kansas; and Representative John Rhodes, an Arizona Republican and former Kansan who is minority leader in the U.S. House, have been among those supporting the appointment of Reilly to the post.

"Reilly is a superb choice for the assignment by virtue of his professional qualifications and his long close ties with Ireland," the editorial concluded.

At any rate, this nomination brought me to the Reagan White House, where actress Maureen O'Hara was a frequent guest. O'Hara was well known for her conservative politics and her support for Republican presidents Dwight D. Eisenhower, Richard Nixon, Gerald Ford, Ronald Reagan, George H. W. Bush and George W. Bush. President Reagan really wanted her to be the ambassador to Ireland, but she made it clear she wouldn't accept, as she didn't want all the social obligations.

One of the brightest stars in Hollywood for decades, Maureen O'Hara costarred with John Wayne in five films, including *The Quiet Man* in 1952. I mention this movie in particular because of a meeting I had later with this great lady. We kept in touch occasionally after that initial meeting, and some time later, I visited County Cork, where she lived at Lugdine Park.

I was in Ireland staying with two friends, Paul Giddens and Fred Wyrsch. The three of us were staying on a beautiful farm owned by twin priests who served in Tonganoxie and Lawrence. During that time, we went to the village where Maureen lived, and she extended the invitation for an Irish tea. I was the only one of us who went back to her residence, and at one point, she invited me up to her bedroom.

I didn't know what to think. Under normal circumstances, you'd be happy to escort Maureen O'Hara to her bedroom. But when we got there, I saw a quilt rack adorned by a cape at the end of her bed. She said, "Do you know *The Quiet Man*?"

I said, "My God, is this that cape?" She said yes, and she took it off the rack and put it on my shoulders. She told me I was only the second man upon whom she'd placed that cape. This touched me immensely, since I know what great friends the two of them were.

They were such good friends, in fact, that shortly before Wayne's death in 1979, Maureen testified before a House subcommittee asking that the president strike a commemorative coin that read, "John Wayne, American." Her testimony is outlined in a 2007 article in *Cowboys and Indians,* known as the "Premier Magazine of the West." The coin was struck.

Also in the 1980s, I was to meet the famous athlete Muhammad Ali at a GOP convention in Louisville, Kentucky. There was a lot of Kentucky bourbon flowing at an event hosted by Mitch McConnell. I think it was a State Chamber of Commerce event, as those attending were members of various legislatures. Ali had endorsed Reagan in the 1984 race, a move that surprised many, and I'm sure that's why he was at the convention. I had the opportunity to sip a Kentucky bourbon with the fighter, who was very pleasant and conversational. He showed some signs of Parkinson's disease at the time.

My friendship with the Irish officers led to my last official post, US Observer to the International Fund for Ireland, what you could call my last hurrah. I was appointed in 2019 by the Trump administration and served for about two and a half years. In that role, I visited Ireland and reported to the State Department on programs and how they performed, whether they were successful in keeping the peace between southern and northern Ireland. One effort by the International Peace Fund was to get the North to tear down the barriers in their neighborhoods. Even when I was there, there were still eight-foot-tall fences in beautiful neighborhoods in the North to separate them from their neighbors.

I also made recommendations about funding for future projects to promote peace in this region. During one visit, I attended an International Fund meeting and stayed in Cavan in the Border Region, a town in the South used by people from the North who wanted to stash their weapons in the South during the conflict. The Cavan Museum highlights the part played by both Northern Ireland and the Republic of Ireland in World War I, and I wanted to see how effective the museum was.

I met with fifty master's and doctoral students, twenty-five from the North and twenty-five from the South, and they indicated they weren't in conflict with each other and were way beyond that. The programs promoting peace have focused on anything from sports, to education, to employment skills, to law enforcement efforts. Though there remain old-timers who harbor resentment and have horrible memories of past conflicts, I believe that hatred will eventually subside over time as the new generation comes along.

Because of my earlier visits to Ireland, I, too, have memories of the conflict, particularly since I stayed in areas near the border region. I watched the IRA snatch a guy off the streets in Belturbet, Ireland in the middle of the night. I guess he was an informer or was believed to be one.

I remember hearing him scream, and I heard more noise; it was three thirty in the morning, and I woke up to this. I was on the second floor of this Irish flat on the main street of this village called Belturbet, where we think the Reillys came from. I was the guest of the McDwyers, who had Reilly ancestors.

I went down the next morning for breakfast, and I said, "Mrs. McDwyer, did you hear all that noise and racket last night?" She said she had.

I asked what happened, since I looked out and saw a car and, they were throwing this guy in it. She said, "You'll never know any more about it. That was the IRA." She knew, as they lived right on the border. She said, "That's probably all you're going to hear, Ed, what you saw."

Another really scary thing happened when I was with her son Eamon. He was a physician, well known in that area in County Cavan. Eamon wanted to take me to the North, as he ran back and forth all the time for his practice, and the IRA knew his car and his license plate. So he took me in his Audi to a spot along the coast where there were a lot of generating windmills. We had crossed the border to the North and we were on top of the hill sightseeing.

The next thing Eamon said was, "Oh my God! They're blocking the road."

I said, "What?" He was looking down, and several big tractors with equipment blocked the road. I said, "What's going on?"

He said, "They're checking my car to see who I am. We'll just drive down and get close to where they are. We'll just sit until they open this road. They'll probably let us through. They're really checking the car. Once they figure out I'm not a sympathizer or whatever, they'll probably let us through."

It was an hour and a half or two hours we had to sit and wait before they finally moved the tractors. You weren't going to get out of there otherwise, because the roads were all two-lane pass. When I was an observer, I told several people that story. They said I was lucky. If they didn't know me and hadn't figured out that the doctor had patients in the North, who knows what would have happened.

One thing stood out during my last assignment as US observer to the International Fund for Ireland. Ireland is rapidly becoming a leader in cutting-edge science, research, and other emerging technologies. Since 2019 the Irish have witnessed a 33 percent increase in domestic products, and the country enjoys a reputation as one of the European Union's best performing economies. This is all the more reason to maintain peace between the two Irelands and enhance the future of those in Northern Ireland.

The island has become a haven for international investors, resulting in industries like pharmaceuticals, information, and technology communications as we move away from depending on other nations to provide these services. I often travelled to Ireland in my younger years, and I cannot be happier for the land of our ancestors as I witness its progress. This has been accomplished by realizing that resolution of the conflict between North and South is resulting in even deeper roots with America and a dynamic future for the Irish continent.

Most recently, I've become involved in a group designated as the 13 Club, established within the past year and a half. A major player in that group is Tony R. Culley-Foster, president and CEO of the World Affairs Council and the founder and president of CFCO International. He is renowned as a business leader, lobbyist, and educator, among other accomplishments. He was born in Londonberry, Northern Ireland, and educated in Ireland, England, and the United States.

The 13 Club emphasizes maintaining peace between northern and southern Ireland. Since Brexit, troubles resurfaced because of a detail in the trade agreement that adversely affects Northern Ireland. Called the Northern Ireland Protocol, it was ratified in January 2020, and it stems from the fact that Ireland remains part of the European Union, but Northern Ireland no longer is.

This proved to be a thorny problem for Rishi Sunak, the former British prime minister, who first met with President Joe Biden in November 2022. At that time, he pledged that Britain would settle this trade dispute with the European Union by April 2023, the twenty-fifth anniversary of the Good Friday Agreement that eased tensions between northern and southern Ireland. Most recently, Sunak proposed the creation of a red and green lane, which meant those goods traveling in the green lane would come from trusted traders promising the items are only for Northern Ireland. They would be check-free, versus those in the red lane that would end up in the Republic of Ireland. These goods would be subject to inspection and possibly tariffs. The hope is this may lead to more positive talks with all parties. It has been an added privilege for me to serve the Trump administration as the US Peace Observer for two-plus years in view of my long association with the island of Ireland, home of our ancestors.

As I've reflected on Ireland and what a great opportunity I had, I realize that I was named US Observer to the International Fund for Ireland because I hosted Irish officers attending the Command and General Staff College. Ireland, like America, has its challenges with the immigration issue and the loss of some of their identity. The people remain restless, and it bodes of a time in history when we sought leaders with courage and integrity. We must have this if we are to regain the trust of those we serve.

To see some of our elected representatives today selling to or engaging with those who are not necessarily friends of America is not only a disgrace, it's treason and a violation of the oath of office they took:

> I do solemnly swear (or affirm) that I will support and defend the Constitution of the United States against all enemies, foreign and domestic; that I will bear true faith and allegiance to the same; that I take this obligation freely, without any mental reservation or purpose of evasion; and that I will well and faithfully discharge the duties of the office on which I am about to enter: So help me God.

On another note, coming to the nation's capital also afforded me the opportunity to extend my knowledge and service not only to the criminal justice system, but also to religious organizations. These include the

Knights of Malta and the Knights of the Holy Sepulchre, both of which support the poor and sick.

It's also given me a chance to serve on the boards of the American University of Rome and the Institute of World Politics. I am currently vice chairman of the board of trustees for the Institute. At the Institute, a graduate school of national security, intelligence, and international affairs, we are committed to developing leaders with a sound understanding of international realities and the ethical conduct of statecraft. We believe that should be based on knowledge and appreciation of the founding principles of the American political economy and the Western moral tradition.

We pride ourselves on having some of the best instructors in the world in their respective fields. It has been a privilege to serve in this great cause the Institute embodies to help achieve peace, freedom, security, and prosperity of our constitutional republic. This is done while minimizing the loss of precious blood and lives through war and conflicts.

I was extremely fortunate to meet Dr. John Lenzcowski, founder of the IWP. He was in the State Department under the Reagan administration. The IWP has instilled in me through its work a greater faith and appreciation of what our founding fathers believed. It confirms for me that faith and a spiritual foundation in Judeo-Christian principles is what makes this the greatest nation on earth.

Now as I reflect in my current assignment as IWP board of trustees vice president, I recognize the part we are playing in ensuring the future security of our country. The students we graduate are tangible evidence of the Institute's impact as they embark on careers in the federal system.

My parents influenced my education and faith by placing me in the hands of the Sisters of Charity for eight of my formative years. That faith and training have guided me in my professional decisions, some of which have life and death impacts for others. That has given me comfort in presiding over the US Parole Commission after serving in the Kansas Legislature.

What the future holds for those who follow us is frightening, but just as we had to adapt to the challenges presented, I am confident they, too, will work to preserve and protect the republic. IWP is just another instrument to ensure that happens. And though I am aging in body, I am committing my life in these senior years to continue serving in whatever capacity I can to give back for the many blessings and opportunities I have received in life.

19

Ten Masters

Since I was sworn into the Kansas Legislature in 1963, I have served in the administrations of ten governors and presidents, whom I have referred to as my ten Masters. I will start with President Ronald Reagan, though I was not picked for the first position for which I was nominated during his administration.

Ronald Reagan, Elected President November 4, 1980

This was an interesting time in my life, as I'd spent twenty-plus years in the Legislature and supported Reagan but was not a major contributor. In spite of that, Senator Bob Dole and others went to bat for me in seeking consideration for an appointment as ambassador to Ireland, considering all the Irish families I had sponsored at Fort Leavenworth. There was one caveat I would add today, and that is I was an Irish bachelor, since I didn't tie the knot with Luci until May 16, 1986. Senator Dole indicated they'd be most apt to appoint a bachelor who was well known in Ireland. After all, I even judged the "Rose of Tralee" beauty contest one year when I was a young senator from Kansas.

I suppose I was naïve but truly committed, and I was elevated to one of five on the list. The number one was a road contractor whose contracts in highway jobs resulted in a "no way" by the FBI. I presume I cleared that hurdle, as I was among the other four who attended the White House Saint Patrick's luncheon with the newly-elected Taoiseach Charles Haughey and his daughter Eimear, whom I had once dated. At that luncheon my path and that of Maureen O'Hara crossed, and at her request we adjourned to the rose garden at the luncheon's conclusion. The rest is history as we became friends, Maureen told Ronnie she wasn't interested in the ambassadorship, and in the end, none of the remaining four were selected.

Another good friend, former Congresswoman Margaret Heckler, was appointed to the position and did a marvelous job representing the United States. In 1986 Luci and I took an extended honeymoon to Ireland, and we had a personal visit with Margaret in the US ambassador's residence at Phoenix Park. This house was designed by James Hoban, who also designed the US White House. It was a visit neither Luci nor I would ever forget. I appreciated that so many supported me on two occasions for appointment to positions in Ireland. In the end I am grateful President Donald Trump's administration recognized the importance of our International Officers Program at Fort Leavenworth and the good will and support of allies it attracts to the preservation of our nations.

The Reagan presidency brought a new conservative philosophy to the party. He was one of the first true conservative presidents in fifty years. His mission was to advance domestic policies focused on reducing the federal government's role in solving problems and reducing restrictions on business, while implementing tax reduction to stimulate investment and entrepreneurship. He was a fierce opponent of the spread of Communism and definitely distrusted the Soviet Union, which he labeled the Evil Empire. He championed rearming our nation and building a stronger defense. Though I wasn't appointed the new Irish ambassador, I was asked to serve on the National Highway Advisory Committee. I appreciated that, even though Congress abolished it within a year of my appointment. My time upon the stage was brief, and I continued to serve as the Kansas senator from Leavenworth.

Governor John Anderson, January 1961–January 1965

Governor John Anderson swore me into service in the Kansas House in 1963, and I served in his administration for two years. Governor Anderson, the thirty-sixth governor of Kansas, was the state's former attorney general and prior to that, a state senator from Johnson County. Governor Anderson's impact on education reform was significant and included school consolidation. As attorney general and then governor, he was also a strong proponent of capital punishment.

He was also the first governor to move into Cedar Crest, the executive mansion. Anderson and his family moved to that French-Norman style house in 1962 from the first governor's home at Eighth and Buchanan. That home was in disrepair, and Frank and Madge MacLennan's stately house in west Topeka proved to be the perfect executive mansion. Built in 1928, it sits on 244 acres; the hill on which it's located overlooks the Kansas River Valley, and it is filled with cedar trees. While in the Senate, I served on the planning committee for remodeling that home. I became good friends with another committee member, Ruth Stauffer, whose husband was president of Stauffer Communications. Ruth was active in numerous civic and philanthropic activities in Topeka.

Governor William Avery, January 1965–January 1967

It was then on to my dear friend who was also a great friend of my dad, Governor William H. Avery. As a young legislator, I remember the former US House member asking my dad as they were on the reviewing stand at a Leavenworth parade, "Ed, who just went by in that car or float?" He wanted to address that person by first name later. It was a lesson I never forgot—how important it is to remember those you meet, whether it's in business or politics.

Chapter 19

Governor Robert Docking, January 1967–January 1975

Governor Robert Docking entered the fray in January 1967 and served until January 1975. The Democratic governor was a great businessman whose banking career and success were testimony to his ability to run the government well. I had the privilege along with Wyandotte and Johnson County colleagues to introduce him to the private club dilemma prevalent at the time in Kansas. Private clubs operated behind clouded windows and locked doors, and taxpayers should have been collecting some gratuity. Many of their activities violated state statutes.

Governor Docking, whom I'd describe as a man's man, enjoyed those field trips. And as a result, the Legislature passed constitutional amendments. They allowed the state to regulate a totally out-of-control industry that had been breeding a lot of other problems for our state and its reputation.

Governor Robert Bennett, January 1975–January 1979

The election of my colleague in the Senate and friend Governor Robert Bennett brought a professional and all-business administration to the state. Bob served well in the Senate and had a sterling reputation as a guy you could trust. He was a dollar and cents guy who wanted a responsible and sound approach to the state's fiscal needs.

Governor John Carlin, January 1979–January 1987

Governor John W. Carlin was only the second Democratic governor while I was a legislator—George Docking was the first—and Carlin brought western-Kansas thinking to the Statehouse halls. He was easy to visit with but hard to persuade when I urged him not to veto the capital punishment bill the Legislature passed several times under his tenure. He vetoed the bill not once, but four times, in 1979, 1980, 1981, and 1985.

Maybe he failed to remember one of the many terrible crimes committed in Kansas, when the Clutter family living near Holcomb was brutally murdered in November 1959.

Governor Mike Hayden, January 1987–January 1991

Finally, there was Governor Mike Hayden, another farm lad who grew up in the small northwest-Kansas town of Atwood. He was much more sympathetic to the plight some suffer at the hands of those who can't appreciate that everyone is entitled to the right of life, liberty, and the pursuit of happiness. It was in the last year of Mike Hayden's administration that I was nominated by President George H. W. Bush to be appointed and named chairman of the US Parole Commission. This was thanks to the help of my US senators and others who supported my efforts.

President George H. W. Bush, 1989–1993

President Bush appointed and named me chairman, with the urging and endorsement of Senators Bob Dole and Nancy Landon Kassebaum. I was appointed in 1991 and confirmed in August 1992 by the Senate Judiciary Committee chaired by Senator Joe Biden. President Bush, like those who have followed him, expressed what he saw as a chance to "change the tone" in national politics and encourage a more civil discourse. He sought peace when he warned Iraqi President Saddam Hussein about nuclear weapons. Although my service under President Bush was not long, since he was defeated by President Bill Clinton, I found him dedicated to the task which he and First Lady Barbara truly enjoyed. He had the reputation of being a man you could trust.

Chapter 19

President William Jefferson Clinton, 1993–2001

I completed what was to be my five-year appointment, only to be asked by President Clinton to remain on the job. That was because Congress shut down the District of Columbia Lorton prison and moved all its inmates to the federal Bureau of Prisons. Taking over District of Columbia parole cases and closing the local Lorton prison cast a new light on the United States Parole Commission. It meant we inherited some nine thousand local offenders, many of whom were parole eligible.

Clinton was a charismatic, fun-loving president who promised to help the country adapt to a changing world by reducing the deficit, asking the wealthy to pay their fair share, investing in the future, and creating jobs. I found his administration staffed by loyal and devoted appointees; many had served him when he was Arkansas governor. He reappointed me, and my brother-in-law Jim Slattery and my wife Luci played a role in making that happen. So did Saul Stern, a neighbor who was Maryland's biggest Democratic fundraiser.

By chance, we ran into one another as I was leaving the condo, and he asked about my status on the Parole Commission. I told him that because it was slated to close down, I planned to return to Kansas to run for Congress, governor, or lieutenant governor. He said he would check on the Commission's status and asked if I would stay in Washington if it were to remain active. This was about the time closing Lorton prison in DC was being discussed. I said I'd like to remain if the Commission was still going.

Stern sent a personal letter to President Clinton saying he'd like to see Reilly remain as chairman of the Commission. And I did during his first term. To me that was just another example that you never know what impact a person you meet may have on your life's plan.

I enjoyed meeting President Clinton on several occasions, the latest being the funeral of Senator Bob Dole. One of Clinton's priorities was the wise decision to ask former Senator George Mitchell to seek a peace agreement over the Troubles in Northern Ireland, which led to the Good

Friday Agreement. This has allowed peace to prevail over the last twenty-five years after decades of violence.

President George W. Bush, 2001–2009

I was again fortunate George W. Bush asked me to remain as chairman. He didn't make decisions lightly and assembled a cabinet recognized for its overall competence. This included appointing General Colin Powell as the first African American secretary of state. When we dedicated the Buffalo Soldier monument at Fort Leavenworth in 1992, both General Powell and Senator Bob Dole attended. Luci and I hosted them at the beautiful residence of Ed and Rosemary Wettig, a Leavenworth home that resembled the White House.

Like all our presidents, President George W. Bush was faced with crisis, something that seems inevitable to those in that position. They included the September 11, 2001, terrorist attacks, as well as Hurricane Katrina and the financial crisis at the end of his tenure. He was the first Republican president to enjoy a majority in both houses of Congress since Dwight D. Eisenhower, our former beloved president from Kansas.

Thanks to Katja Bullock, a close friend who worked for President Reagan and both Bushes, I had the opportunity on several occasions to visit with the presidents. Katja was known as the housemother of White House interns, whom she ruled with an iron hand; she was also a wonderful and caring instructor for young aspiring politicos. Many of them went on to fill chairs in Congress, state legislatures, or government agencies.

President Donald Trump, 2017–2021

Donald Trump became the forty-fifth president in January 2017, very much as a political outsider. He wanted to change a lot of the past customs and expectations of the presidency, which often prompted headlines and gained him daily public attention. As a former New York businessman, Trump's victory in 2016 defied a lot of the norms of Washington and the political landscape. He and his administration sparked controversy at every turn, and the new president seemed to love a political fight.

He used the media and his microphone to criticize a long list of those whom he thought were adversaries, from the media to members of his own administration. His numerous tweets exposed his thinking on a variety of issues and proved provocative, especially in his final days in office. Like most presidents, he had a vision for America, and his administration achieved a list of long-sought domestic victories including major tax cuts and reshaping the judiciary. Internationally he imposed tougher immigration standards and altered some multilateral agreements.

In his third year as president, I was appointed to the post of US Observer to the International Fund for Ireland. I served the administration in that post for two and a half years, leaving in the first six months of the Biden administration. I'm sure sponsoring seven Irish families who studied at Fort Leavenworth's Command and General Staff College provided significant credentials for this post. It was a privilege to be asked to serve in an effort to support and monitor the Good Friday Agreement.

It should be noted that my appointed post for seven presidents overlapped with the time of election, and I was held over until the new administration appointed a successor. For example, this occurred from George H. W. Bush to Clinton, when I served two terms before my reappointment by George W. Bush, and when I was a holdover for six months in both the Obama and Biden administrations.

* * * * *

Besides presidents and governors, as a state legislator and as US Parole chairman, I had some knowledge of both federal and state attorneys general. As for the federal attorneys general, I can say that all of them followed a hands-off policy when it came to injecting themselves into the parole process for fear of attracting massive media attention claiming they were trying to influence a Commission's decision. The federal statute is clear that the US Parole Commission is accountable as an administrative agency to the Justice Department, but it's hands-off when it comes to the Commission's decisions.

US Attorneys General

- William P. Barr 1991–1993
- Janet Reno 1993–2001
- John D. Ashcroft 2001–2005
- Alberto R. Gonzales 2005–2007
- Judge Michael B. Ukase 2007–2009
- Eric H. Holder 2009–2015 (I left in his first year in the office.)

Kansas Attorneys General

- William M. Ferguson 1961–1965
- Robert C. Londerholm 1965–1969
- Kent Frizell 1969–1971
- Vern Miller 1971–1975
- Curt T. Schneider 1975–1979
- Robert Stephan 1979–1995

I want to mention Attorney General Robert Stephan briefly, since we were close friends, and my service with him with the longest. As the state's longest-serving attorney general, he was a delightful and colorful law and order advocate. We became good friends, and I stayed in contact with him until his untimely passing in January 2023.

He was a champion for children as well as victims of crime, and we often discussed his upbringing in Wichita and his strong sense of doing what is right. His service took him into a period of an increasingly partisan atmosphere affecting the National Association of Attorneys, where he was a leader. I sensed a change in the public discourse in 1992 as I was preparing to leave for Washington as the chairman of the US Parole Commission. We are all now witnessing the lack of civility and respect for the opinion of others and the lack of debate and compromise—and even suppression of speech that impacts our government at many levels.

Whether in business or one of the appointed positions, my mission has always been helping others. That was embedded in me from the days of insurance and real estate when my father was adamant about coming to the aid of someone in need. He sometimes forgave renters who were unable to pay. Some couldn't make a payment on car loans he and his father had made. He was one of the most charitable men I've known, and he spoke often of why it was the responsibility of everyone able to do the same.

As I look back over my years of service, I recognize that we should all be in the business of saving souls. Given that charge we would be well advised to do so, for we will answer to the ultimate Master, regardless of our deeds. The major reason I began this memoir was to remind us that our life should be about accounting to Him.

20

Defenders of the Faith

As I enter my golden years, it becomes even more obvious we will, upon leaving this world, be given an opportunity to account for what we did—or didn't do—in recognizing the needs of others. The critical importance of generosity to the less fortunate is something I learned firsthand from my parents and through a number of religious organizations of which I have been a member over the decades. Spirituality and faith deeply influenced my service as a federal parole official, and prayer played a part in many key decisions.

Growing up in a Catholic family had a great influence on my life, as did my early education. Attending a Catholic school during most of the years prior to high school helped shape many of my beliefs and principles. I know that spiritual connection played a tremendous role in helping me cope with the loss of my beloved wife Luci soon after our son Joseph was born and the realization I would be raising him as a single dad.

Participation in several religious orders such as the Sovereign Military Order of Malta, the Equestrian Order of the Holy Sepulchre, and the Sacred Military Order of Saint George has given me several perspectives about our Christian upbringing. They emphasize the dignity of man and the importance of believing everyone is a potential contributor to our society and way of life. The Knights have been significant in the charitable work in which they engage as well as the care of the sick and the poor. Each affiliation has given me new and deeper perspectives about my Christian upbringing and how we as Christians are meant to interact with the broader world, our society, and way of life. All the orders are centered on a charitable purpose and committed to the care of the less fortunate.

In a recent conversation with a new friend, the topic of Shriners came up. and he asked if I'd ever thought about becoming a Shriner. It reminded me that my father, with his Ed Reilly Orchestra, played at many of the Shrine dances in the grand upstairs hall on Delaware Street, as Leavenworth was one of the largest chapters. He worked his way through law school with that orchestra.

The talk reminded me that at one point in my life, early on in my legislative career, I considered membership in the Shriners, partly as a way to increase my desire to serve others. But I knew the Church opposed such membership, since the Shrine, as well as some other fraternal orders, was considered a secretive organization that conducted secret rituals and required memorizing a great deal of regalia. I took the liberty of writing a letter to Archbishop Edward Joseph Hunkeler, who was the archbishop of Kansas City in Kansas. I told him I was looking into the opportunity of joining, and I wondered why Catholics weren't supposed to join the Shrine. Three or four weeks later, I got a letter from him that I still have. He wrote, and I paraphrase, "Ed, I so appreciate you writing and asking me if you could join the Shrine, a secretive Masonic order." I knew that several presidents had been members. He added that he found nothing "that directly prevents you from joining, in my opinion." He did ask that I let him know in advance if I decided to join.

Leavenworth resident Merle Euler, a leader in the local Shrine, had encouraged me to join, and I'd asked him about learning the oaths and orders. As it happened, I'd just finished the process of becoming an Exalted Ruler of the Elks Club, and I decided not to join the Shriners. To me, it was another test in the ability to sort out what organizations to join and avoiding groups that might discriminate against people's rights to make decisions.

Knights and Dames of the Holy Order of Malta are servants of the poor and sick whom we consider as belonging to our Lord. We are often referred to as the Defenders of the Faith, a reference to all who through their faith believe and practice what the greatest document, the Bible, teaches those who read it and live by its word. Prior to my appointment to the US Parole Commission and living in the nation's capital, I met Dr. Tom Melady at a GOP convention in Florida. He became a close friend, and he was also a great support to me as a member of Malta. Dr. Melady went on to become the ambassador to Burundi and later the Vatican. His wife Margaret became president of the Federal Association of Malta.

But several others were paramount in sponsoring and supporting me through my investiture into the Order of Malta. Investiture into the Order of Malta is a solemn ceremony that marks the admission of new members into the Order. The candidates for admission to the Order participate in a year of formation, during which they learn the history and spirituality of the Order, among other things. A bachelor attorney I knew, Joe Ryan, was my sponsor when my journey into the Order began. After his passing, Judge Jim and Barbara Murphy took over that role.

In the Knights of Malta investiture, we received and had to memorize the Daily Prayers of Malta, which I have recited since 1995. This is the prayer:

> *Lord Jesus, Thou has seen fit to enlist me for Thy service amongst the Knights and Dames of St. John of Jerusalem. I humbly entreat Thee through the intercession of the most holy Virgin of Philerme, of St. John the Baptist, Blessed Gerard and all the saints, to keep me faithful to the traditions of our Order. Be it mine to practice and defend the Catholic, the Apostolic, the Roman faith against the enemies of religion, be it mine to practice charity towards my neighbors, especially the poor and sick. Give me the strength I need to carry out this my resolve, forgetful of myself, learning ever from Thy Holy Gospel a spirit of deep and generous Christian devotion, striving ever to promote God's glory, the world's peace, and all that may benefit the Order of St. John of Jerusalem.*
>   *Amen.*

I believe as I look back and reflect on how I performed, my life centered on the wonderful religious and public education I was blessed to receive. Great influences later in my life were my introduction and invitation from the Knights of Columbus and working for the Fourth Degree status. Membership in the Fourth Degree allows a Knight to display pride in his country, while continuing to serve his community and church. The Knights stressed service to others and support of those less fortunate while never forgetting the obligation of raising and nurturing the children we bring into the world.

The Order of Malta was an extension of that mission since we believe the poor and sick belong to our Lord. If you don't accept that mission, then you have no place in a lay order that is engaged in so many aspects of others' lives. This also proved to me that public service was a further recognition that we are here to live our lives, but also to recognize not all are as blessed as some of us.

The Equestrian Order of Sepulchre stresses that one who belongs is a jewel to one's community by living an exemplary Christian life. It testifies to Christian love by supporting works in the Holy Land and preserving the birthplace of Jesus.

The Constantinian Order of Saint George, believed to be the most ancient of the Catholic orders, has from its earliest origins supported the glorification of the Cross. It also supports the propagation of the Faith and the defense of the Holy Roman Church. It dedicates itself to the two greatest and most important social works, hospital assistance and charity.

The religious orders I belong to have influenced me to remember with humility the plight of others, be they poor, sick, or serving time in prison. That service welded in me the need to look to others with dignity, compassion, and concern for their welfare. My father, who was a servant in his own right, was fond of telling me, "You are blessed, Ed, but you must remember many are not, and it's your responsibility never to forget that."

I know both of my parents served through their generosity and philanthropy to others less fortunate, and my brother Jerry has done so as well. I'm convinced it was their example that led me to the public square as an insurance and real estate broker, legislator, and ultimately as chairman of the United States Parole Commission and a US Observer to the International Fund for Ireland. All of it made possible the ultimate service I have been able to give back, serving the great people of Kansas, the United States, and the people of Ireland. It has been a marvelous life enhanced by the satisfaction that came from trying to be of service to whoever asked and some who never did.

Interestingly enough, my first exposure to Washington, DC, resulted from a spiritual event. In the mid-fifties, when I was either a senior in high school or a KU freshman, United States Senator Frank Carlson from Kansas invited me to the National Prayer Breakfast. At that time it was held at the Mayflower Hotel.

Another Kansan, President Dwight D. Eisenhower, was the first president to attend the prayer breakfast in 1953. Credit for the gathering goes to a Norwegian immigrant and Methodist Minister, Abraham Vereide, who lived in Seattle in the 1930s. He organized local groups of politicians and businessmen to talk and pray together before work. Other cities followed that lead, and when Vereide moved to Washington, DC, in 1942, he started breakfast prayer groups for House and Senate members. Carlson, a close friend and adviser to Eisenhower, attended one of the prayer groups. Through Carlson the 1953 breakfast connected the House, Senate, and president.

President Ronald Reagan, the keynote speaker at the 1986 National Prayer Breakfast, said Eisenhower told Carlson the White House was the "loneliest house he'd ever been in," according to *Time Magazine's History Newsletter*. Carlson suggested the president attend his prayer group, and when he did, it was the first joint prayer breakfast. When President Eisenhower spoke at that first prayer breakfast—known as the Presidential Prayer Breakfast until 1970—he talked of the role of religion in founding the United States and the necessity of prayer in his own time.

I regularly attend the prayer breakfast, which is now held at the Hilton Hotel where President Reagan was shot. Since that shooting, security is intensive; the President and First Lady always attend the event, which is the first Thursday in February. They are escorted in through a secure garage built after the assassination attempt. More than four thousand people now attend the annual breakfast, coming from all over the world and from all denominations. I have met kings, princesses, and presidents of other nations there.

My first breakfast was either in 1955 or 1957, and it led to an even deeper friendship with Senator Carlson. I'd met him because he was involved in watershed dam projects that resulted in the building of Yllier Lake—Reilly spelled backwards. I've already registered for the 2024 breakfast, which will mark over fifty that I've attended. Without question, the faith expressed at all these breakfasts has been a further influence on my own faith and the advocacy of serving others in whatever ways we can.

Now there's also a National Catholic Prayer Breakfast in Washington, DC, established in 2004. I have attended three of these assemblies, which bring a variety of religions together and also involve workshops. I'm convinced bringing together people of all religious denominations and political parties is another opportunity to civilly and peacefully resolve many differences in today's society. It may be the only way we can resolve some of the world issues for those honestly committed to work for peace and solidarity among people.

Looking at our challenges today, I reflect on those years of service. I pray for the day that the next generation can chart a new era of brotherhood in this nation. We have to recognize the right of others to their opinions, and we have to respect others. I urge our religious and political leaders to work together in charting that course.

What a day it will be when we can eliminate intolerance and bitterness toward one another. Only then can we live together as equals in the harmony and peace we need to leave for others. Whatever I may have contributed to this effort during my years, I am grateful to the citizens of Kansas and America for making it possible.

All my public service has been an education no money could buy. It's all about recognizing and giving back. Some of the people I have worked with over the years have been kind enough to say they think I have done this. In a July 2023 interview, former hearing examiner Joe Pacholski observed, "Ed is an unusual individual in that the core values from his faith dictate his endeavors as he goes forward. I really do believe he tries to give back; that's what he practices."

As I complete this work that has taken many years of recalling events that shaped my life, I have tried to share my good fortune while trying to make sure my son Joe is settled in life and pursuing a career that he can build on. When he came into our lives, I realized I had the responsibility of raising him as a single father and encouraging him to build on the reputation for which I'm grateful. I have stressed to him his obligation to give back, because that's what has driven me in doing whatever I could to ensure American freedom and opportunity. I am hopeful he will work toward making our nation more successful by his efforts to eliminate discrimination and hatred. If he can also help improve a criminal justice system that's always in need of revision, he will have accomplished all we can expect.

As we learn in Luke 12:48, "To whom much is given, much is required." Our job in life is to find our passion and mold and direct it in a way that positively impacts the lives of others. This has been one of my key takeaways from faith, and that reality has helped to drive humanity forward.

I'm also reminded of a quote I try to say daily: "To have faith is to have wings. Every day is a fresh beginning. Every morning is the world made new."

Acknowledgments

These people and documents have been instrumental in writing this autobiography, and I want to extend my thanks.

Paul Feliciano; Ramon Powers; Debra Bates-Lamborn; Terry Campbell; Jerry Collins; Davis Moulden; Mary Ann Corominas; *The Leavenworth Times*; Charles McAtee; *Fresh Hell* podcast, 2022, Episode 175; *The Lawrence Journal-World*; *The Wichita Eagle*; Kerri Rawson, *A Serial Killer's Daughter*; Larry Welch, *Beyond Cold Blood: The KBI from Ma Barker to BTK*; Candice DeLong, *Killer Psyche* podcast, 2022, "The Wichita Massacre."

Ann Foster; Mike Gaines; Jim Slattery; Louis Klemp; *The Kansas City Star*; *The Leavenworth Post*; The Kansas State Historical Society; Nedra Spingler; Deanna Willard; Sebastian Smeareann; Jerry Reilly; Bill Clinton; Janet Reno; Emory Cox; Joe Pacholski; Cindee Jacobs; Joseph Reilly; Strom Thurmond; Michael and Mae Gannon; Peter Hoffman; Jasper Clay; Cranston Mitchell; Tom Hutchinson; James Johnston; Monica David Morris; *The Beacon*, November 2023; *The Kansas City Times*; *Cowboys and Indians* magazine, 2007 edition; and *Time* magazine's "History" Newsletter.

www.ingramcontent.com/pod-product-compliance
Lightning Source LLC
Chambersburg PA
CBHW020540030426
42337CB00013B/915